CHILDREN'S FICTION
1765–1808

John Carey
Margaret King Moore, Lady Mount Cashell
Henry Brooke

edited with an introduction and notes by
Anne Markey

FOUR COURTS PRESS

Set in 10.5 pt on 12.5 pt Bembo for
FOUR COURTS PRESS LTD
7 Malpas Street, Dublin 8, Ireland
www.fourcourtspress.ie
and in North America for
FOUR COURTS PRESS
c/o ISBS, 920 N.E. 58th Avenue, Suite 300, Portland, OR 97213.

A catalogue record for this title
is available from the British Library.

ISBN 978–1–84682–287–2 hbk
978–1–84682–288–9 pbk

Printed in England
by CPI Antony Rowe, Chippenham, Wilts.

Contents

The Literature of Early Modern Ireland series

Previously published in the series:
Faithful Teate, *Ter Tria*, ed. Angelina Lynch (2007)
Henry Burkhead, *Cola's Furie* (1646), ed. Angelina Lynch and Patricia Coughlan (2009)
Richard Nugent, *Cynthia* (1604), ed. Angelina Lynch and Anne Fogarty (2010)
William Dunkin, *The Parson's Revels*, ed. Catherine Skeen (2010)

Early Irish Fiction, *c*.1680–1820

Also in the series:
[Anon], *Virtue Rewarded; or, The Irish Princess*, ed. Ian Campbell Ross and Anne Markey (2010)
Sarah Butler, *Irish Tales*, ed. Ian Campbell Ross, Aileen Douglas, & Anne Markey
Thomas Amory, *The Life of John Buncle, Esq.*, ed. Moyra Haslett (2011)
Elizabeth Sheridan, *The Triumph of Prudence over Passion*, ed. Aileen Douglas and Ian Campbell Ross (2011)

Forthcoming in the series:
Charles Johnstone, *The History of Arsaces, Prince of Betlis*, ed. Daniel Sanjiv Roberts (2012)

Preface

Irish prose fiction of the long eighteenth century has only recently begun to receive the attention it merits. While such names as Swift, Goldsmith and Edgeworth have long been familiar to readers of Irish (and British) literature, many other writers – born, educated, or living in Ireland – produced a substantial and imaginatively varied body of fiction from the late-seventeenth to the early-nineteenth century. This series aims more fully to indicate the diversity and breadth of Irish literature in the period 1680–1820 by providing critical editions of a range of exemplary works of prose fiction. In so doing, it will indicate the role the early novel played in inventing Ireland for readers at home and abroad, while offering new perspectives on the literature and history of these islands.

Each title in the series will contain a carefully-edited text, together with a critical introduction, a select bibliography, and comprehensive notes, designed for scholars and students of Irish writing in English, of the English novel, and all those concerned with Ireland c.1680–c.1820.

Aileen Douglas
Moyra Haslett
Ian Campbell Ross

Acknowledgments

The editor gratefully acknowledges financial assistance from the Centre for Irish-Scottish and Comparative Studies, Trinity College Dublin. For their advice and assistance at all stages, the editor is grateful to Ian Campbell Ross, Aileen Douglas and Moyra Haslett. For their generosity in answering queries, I am also grateful to Pamela Clemit, Niall Gillespie, Jarlath Killeen, David O'Shaughnessy, AnnaLee Pauls and Sally Williams. Thanks are also due to Claire Markey and Alison Markey for help with proofreading.

The illustration of the frontispiece from the first edition of *Stories of Old Daniel; or, Tales of Wonder and Delight* (1808) is reproduced by permission of the British Library.

The frontispiece illustration from the second edition of *Stories of Old Daniel; or, Tales of Wonder and Delight* (1810) is reproduced by permission of the Board of Trinity College Dublin.

The six illustrations from the second edition of *Learning better than House and Land, as exemplified in the History of Harry Johnson and Dick Hobson* (1810) are reproduced by permission of the Board of Trinity College Dublin.

Introduction

Children's fiction became a recognizable form of writing over the course of the long eighteenth century, during which period the novel established itself as the most influential and popular form of prose literature. Explicitly contrasted, yet displaying close affinities, with texts addressed to adults, children's literature is defined, not by its content, form, authorship, place or period of production, but by its intended readership. While prose fiction, in common with other forms of writing produced by children, is described, and often dismissed, as juvenilia, children's fiction consists of a body of imaginative works produced by adults for younger readers. Until the 1970s, such works were rarely subjected to critical scrutiny, but following the adoption of 'Children's Literature' as a division of the Modern Language Association in 1980, their value has increasingly been recognized. Substantial attention has been paid in recent years to the emergence of English-language children's fiction as a significant site of cultural production that reflected broader adult anxieties and social concerns over the course of the long eighteenth century.[1] Very little research, however, has been undertaken into the Irish dimensions of this topic. As a result, texts written for young readers by Irish authors during the period have received scant attention from critics of either children's literature or early Irish fiction.

Maria Edgeworth (1767–1849) is the only Irish writer of early children's fiction to have attracted sustained and informed critical commentary.[2] As a result, her important contribution to the development of English-language children's fiction has been long and justly recognized, although commentators on children's literature generally place little emphasis on her Irish background.[3] Yet if

---

1 See, for example, Anja Müller (ed.), *Fashioning Childhood in the Eighteenth Century* (Aldershot: Ashgate, 2006) and Mary Hilton and Jill Sheffrin (eds), *Educating the Child in Enlightenment Britain* (Aldershot: Ashgate, 2009).

2 Edgeworth's children's fiction began with *The Parent's Assistant* (1796), followed by other collections of stories, including *Early Lessons* (1801), *Moral Tales* (1801), and *Harry and Lucy Concluded* (1809), as well as *Orlandino* (1848), a novel published the year before her death.

3 See, for example, Mark D. Hawthorne, *Doubt and Dogma in Maria Edgeworth* (Gainesville, FL, 1967), pp 23–38; Mitzi Myers, 'The Dilemmas of Gender as Double-Voiced Narrative; or, Maria Edgeworth Mothers the *Bildungsroman'*, in Robert W. Uphaus (ed.), *The Idea of the Novel in the Eighteenth Century* (East Lansing: Colleagues; Woodbridge: Colleagues Press, 1988), pp 67–96; Sharon Murphy, *Maria Edgeworth and Romance* (Dublin: Four Courts Press, 2002), pp 43–70.

by far the best known Irish author of children's fiction in the late-eighteenth and early-nineteenth centuries, Maria Edgeworth was by no means the only such writer, or even the first. As early as 1765, for example, Henry Brooke (1703–83) included an original fable in the opening volume of *The Fool of Quality; or, The History of Henry, Earl of Moreland* (1765) that was reproduced, for over a hundred years, in texts primarily addressed to young readers. One of these texts was the earliest-known Dublin printed book for children written by an Irishman, *The History of Harry Spencer; compiled for the amusement of good children; and the instruction of such as wish to become good*, which appeared under the pseudonym of 'Philanthropos' in 1794. In order to encourage and facilitate further research into Irish children's fiction of the late-eighteenth and early-nineteenth centuries, the present volume offers a selection of stories, written by Irish authors and published between 1765 and 1808, that were read by, or to, young readers.

The first is a short novel by John Carey, *Learning better than House and Land*, published in London in 1808. This is followed by *Stories of Old Daniel; or, Tales of Wonder and Delight*, a collection of moral tales published anonymously in London that same year and later revealed to be the work of Margaret King Moore, Lady Mount Cashell. Three versions of Henry Brooke's fable conclude the volume. Offering variety in content, genre and style, the texts provide intriguing insights into the Irish contribution to the development of children's literature, both complementing and complicating existing critical approaches to that body of writing. Critics increasingly accept that children's fiction displays national variations, and that these differences can challenge the ways in which this branch of literature is theorized. Contesting 'the notion that there is a "common" children's literature in all countries in the world', Maria Nikolajeva claimed: 'With very few exceptions, children's literature in different countries has little in common'.[4] Emer O'Sullivan has argued that 'Irish children's literature in English is an example of a development influenced by conditions other than those crucial to most other European children's literatures'.[5] Although O'Sullivan justified this claim with reference to twentieth-century Irish writers and cultural conditions, it is equally applicable to texts produced in the long eighteenth century. The work of Irish writers of early children's fiction not only provides general insights into the early development of that form of literature but also illuminates specific national concerns and anxieties.

One such writer was the Dublin born writer, John Carey (1756–1829).[6] His father, Christopher, was a prosperous Roman Catholic baker, who had a con-

---

4   Maria Nikolajeva, *Children's Literature comes of Age: towards a new aesthetic* (New York: Garland, 1996), p. 43.

5   Emer O'Sullivan, *Comparative Children's Literature* (London: Routledge, 2005), p. 57.

6   Following the information given in Leslie Stephen's *Dictionary of National Biography*, vol. IX (London: Smith, Elder, & Co., 1887), p. 73, the date of Carey's death is now universally given as 1826. However, an obituary that appeared in the *Gentleman's Magazine*, April 1830, 376, claimed that Carey died on 8 December 1829, at the age of seventy-three. This later date was

tract with the Royal Navy during the American War of Independence (1775–83).[7] Known details of John Carey's life are sketchy, but he is said to have been sent at the age of twelve to study in France, completing his education at the University of Paris in 1776.[8] Under the restrictions imposed by the Penal Laws, passed by the Irish parliament following the Williamite victory of 1691, not only were Catholics prohibited from participation in political life but also the education of Catholic minors was outlawed. Although the ban on education abroad was not lifted until 1782, the Carey family, like others who could afford that option, must have thought the advantages outweighed the risk. By 1783, reflecting the relaxation of the Penal Laws, John Carey was back in Dublin, running a school in Dorset Street, in the north of the city, an experience that led him to publish a plan for the reformation of Irish education in 1787.[9] Two years later, he visited Philadelphia, where he initially worked with his brother Mathew (1760–1839), the influential publisher and philanthropist who had fled to America in 1784 under threat of prosecution for urging parliamentary reform and repeal of the Penal Laws. Richard Cargill Cole noted: 'John Carey was working as a bookseller in Philadelphia between the years 1791–3, though apparently not at his brother's firm'.[10] During this period, he edited George Washington's official correspondence, which was published in London in 1795.[11] By that time, Carey had settled in London, where he went on to enjoy a successful career as a private tutor and classical scholar, publishing numerous Latin textbooks, which were frequently reprinted.[12] He also wrote children's fiction,

confirmed by Carey's niece, the poet Elizabeth Sheridan Carey, in a memoir of her father, the art critic William Paulet Carey (1759–1839), 'Seventy-nine': or, Brief memoranda illustrative of the two closing years of the life of the late William Carey (Sheffield, 1841), p. 10.

7   Michael Durey, 'The Dublin Society of United Irishmen and the politics of the Carey–Drennan dispute, 1792–1794', Historical Journal, 37:1 (1994), 89–111 (92).

8   See C.W. Sutton, 'Carey, John (1756–1826)', rev. Philip Carter, Oxford Dictionary of National Biography, Oxford University Press, 2004, http://www.oxforddnb.com/view/article/4654, accessed 6 Sept. 2010; Edward C. Carter II, 'Mathew Carey in Ireland, 1760–1784', Catholic Historical Review, 51:4 (1966), 503–27 (505).

9   See John Carey, Sketch of a plan for the reformation of the grammar-schools of Dublin, humbly submitted to the consideration of the Right Hon. and Hon. the Lords & Commons of Ireland (Dublin, 1787).

10 Richard Cargill Cole, Irish Booksellers and English Writers, 1740–1800 (London: Mansell, 1986), p. 52.

11 George Washington, Official letters to the Honorable American Congress: written, during the war between the united colonies and Great Britain by His Excellency George Washington, commander in chief of the continental forces, now President of the United States; Copied by special permission, from the original papers preserved in the Office of the Secretary of State, Philadelphia, ed. John Carey (London, 1795).

12 These included: Latin Prosody made easy; or, Rules and Authorities for the Quantity of final Syllables in general, and of the Increments of Nouns and Verbs interspersed with occasional Observations and Conjectures on the Pronunciation of the ancient Greeks and Romans, to which are added Directions for scanning and composing different Kinds of Verse, followed by analytic Remarks on the Harmonious Structure of the Hexameter, together with Synoptic Tables of Quantity for every Declension and

beginning with *Profitable Amusement for Children; or, Puerile tales, uniting Instruction with Entertainment*, first published anonymously in 1802.[13] This was followed in 1808 by a very successful novel for children, *Learning better than House and Land, as exemplified in the History of a 'Squire and a Cow-herd*, which went into further, slightly emended, editions in 1810, 1813 and *c.*1824, being reissued again in 1864.[14] An occasional contributor to the *Monthly Magazine*, Carey is also reputed to have edited *The Universal Review*, a magazine founded by Richard Phillips in 1824 that ceased publication the following year.[15] Carey died in 1829, the year in which Catholic emancipation was granted by the Westminster parliament. His niece, Elizabeth Sheridan Carey, reported that he was survived by his second wife, Joanna Carey, the author of *Lasting Impressions*, a three-volume novel published in London in 1824, and by their ten-year-old son, who died tragically in 1836. As a classical scholar, John Carey has enjoyed, at least to some degree, the 'lasting reputation' that his niece believed was his due.[16]

By contrast, his role as an author of children's fiction has been almost entirely forgotten. That is perhaps understandable in relation to *Profitable Amusement for Children*, initially published anonymously and described by a contemporary critic as a collection of 'instructive tales, particularly adapted to children in the lower and middle classes of life'.[17] At the expense of narrative interest, these tales, which unfold within domestic settings, endorse such values as diligence, obedience, kindness and self-denial – values that increasingly became associated with nineteenth-century, middle-class morality. *Learning better than House and Land* is of a different order, though, because its advocacy of diligent study is embedded in two contrasting rags-to-riches and riches-to-rags stories that include accounts of a disastrous Chancery suit, two transatlantic voyages, the capture and dissection of a shark, and the misadventures of a drunken American clerk. As one reviewer noted: 'This little tale, or narrative, inculcates the best moral principles, and is sufficiently interesting to attract the attention of youth'.[18] Another critic suggested that *Learning better than House and Land* was 'a counterpart of the old story of the Basket-maker', which recounts how an arrogant rich man is brought to see the error of his ways by a humble craftsman.[19] This tale, purportedly

Conjugation (London, 1800. 1808, and 1818); *An Abridgement of Ainsworth's Latin Dictionary, Designed for the Use of Schools* (London, 1821 and Edinburgh, 1825).

13 This work was reissued as *Profitable Amusement for Children; or, Familiar Tales, combining useful Instruction with pleasing Entertainment*, by the Author of *'Learning better than House and Land'* (London, 1818).

14 The editions of 1810, 1813, *c.*1824, and 1864 had the slightly different subtitle of 'as exemplified in the History of Harry Johnson and Dick Hobson'.

15 Clement King Shorter, *George Borrow and his circle: wherein may be found many hitherto unpublished letters of Borrow and his friends* (London, New York: Routledge, 1913), p. 99.

16 Elizabeth Sheridan Carey, *Seventy-nine*, p. 10.

17 *Literary Panorama and National Register* (March 1819), 234.

18 *Anti-Jacobin Review* (November 1808), 311.

19 *The Monthly Review* (January 1810), 101.

found in a Peruvian manuscript, first appeared in the *Gentleman's Magazine* in 1736, and was later adapted by Ann Fisher in *The Pleasing Instructor* (1756), and by Thomas Day in the first volume of *The History of Sandford and Merton, A Work intended for the Use of Children* (1783–89).²⁰ Carey's novel certainly criticizes aristocratic improvidence and idleness, but here the focus is on the contrasting experiences of two children. Harry Johnson, the spoilt son of a Yorkshire landowner neglects his studies, while Dick Hobson, the son of Mr Johnson's cowherd, diligently attends to his lessons in the village school. When the two eventually find themselves orphaned in America, Johnson's ignorance renders him fit only for the lowly occupation of a barber. By contrast, Hobson's education enables him to become a rich merchant. A similar emphasis on the moral superiority of a farmer's hardy son over the more effete son of a local landowner had been a feature of the framing story of *The History of Sandford and Merton* (1783–9), a work that was inspired by Henry Brooke's description of the contrasting upbringing of two brothers in the first of the five volumes of *The Fool of Quality; or, the History of Henry, Earl of Moreland* (1765–70).

If the contrast between the squire's idle son and the cowherd's studious one was to some degree familiar to adult and young readers, so too was the model of social advancement through literacy, which was a feature of Samuel Richardson's hugely popular novel, *Pamela; or, Virtue Rewarded* (1740), and of the equally successful anonymously authored children's story, *The History of Little Goody Two-Shoes* (1765). Carey's relocation of the two boys to America, however, yielded instructional narrative opportunities that were unusual in children's fiction of the period which, as M.O. Grenby has pointed out, generally favoured 'domestic settings and affluent characters, rather than protagonists carving out their own economic destinies'.²¹ By shifting the action from England to America and orphaning the two central characters of *Learning better than House and Land*, Carey removes them from the confines of domesticity and exposes them to the vagaries of an uncertain economic future. The accounts of the two transatlantic voyages include descriptions of a school of porpoises (p. 58), the phenomenon of the marine rainbow (p. 41), and an experiment that demonstrated the correlation between water pressure and sea depth (pp 41–2). Young readers, then, were provided with incidental lessons in marine biology, meteorology and physics. The vessel on which Harry Johnson is travelling springs a leak in the middle of the Atlantic Ocean and seems likely to sink; the vessel on which Dick Hobson is travelling is smashed to pieces within sight of the American coast by

20 *The Gentleman's Magazine* (January 1736), 11–12; Ann Fisher, *The Pleasing Instructor; or, Entertaining Moralist* (London, 1756), pp 21–6; Thomas Day, *The History of Sandford and Merton*, ed. Stephen Bending and Stephen Bygrave (Peterborough, ON: Broadview Press, 2009), pp 70–4.

21 M.O. Grenby, 'Early British Children's Books: Towards an Understanding of their Users and Usage', *Corvey Women Writers on the Web* at http://www2.shu.ac.uk/corvey/cw3journal/issuethree/grenby.html accessed 18 September 2010.

an unexpected storm. The near disaster and actual shipwreck alert Carey's readers to the very real dangers of sea travel, a topic to which he had previously drawn attention in the *Monthly Magazine*.[22] Once Harry and Dick set foot on dry land, Carey takes every opportunity to demonstrate not only the benefits of education, honesty and hard work, but also the advantages of an egalitarian society that rewards those qualities by offering opportunities for advancement to worthy individuals.

In the first edition of *Learning better than House and Land*, Carey's valorization of American meritocracy over the English system of inherited privilege is exemplified in the contrasting experiences of Dick Hobson and Harry Johnson. On his own initiative, young Dick finds employment in a mercantile firm where he soon works his way up to become a partner, and marries his former employer's daughter. Despite his early advantages, young Johnson has to rely on the good offices of a kindly American clergyman to secure employment as a humble barber who ends up shaving the prosperous son of his father's former cowherd. The political undertones of the story escaped contemporary reviewers who praised the novel for its inculcation of moral principles. As a marketing ploy, condensed versions of two reviews were included in the prefatory material of the 1810 and 1813 editions (see below 'Notes', p. 170). However, while the text of the 1810 edition exactly followed the first edition, later editions contained significant additions that considerably enhanced Carey's subversive endorsement of American values (see below 'Notes', pp 178–9). In both the 1813 edition and the undated fourth edition, Dick Hobson not only becomes a rich merchant but is also elected to Congress, an outcome that in all editions Harry's father had fondly imagined would await his posterity. That a poor boy who, like so many eighteenth-century Irish emigrants, including Mathew Carey, travelled to the United States in the steerage compartment of a ship, becomes a respected member of Congress, suggests that John Carey enthusiastically approved the American commitment to advancement based on individual effort and ability, also sharing his brother's disapproval of English political injustice, as exemplified in the Penal Laws.[23] A comment in the fourth edition, in which Carey observes that 'the American Constitution admits no distinction on account of religion; but with an enlightened and liberal policy, has left even the highest offices in the republic equally accessible to men of every persuasion', supports that suggestion.[24] So too do footnotes in which Carey expressed his support for '*universal religious equality*, which I have long and ardently wished to

---

22 Sutton, 'Carey, John (1756–1826)', reports: 'In the latter journal [*Monthly Magazine*] (1803) he made a suggestion for enabling persons on shore to give assistance to distressed vessels by shooting a wooden ball from a mortar, an idea subsequently conceived and carried out independently by George Manby, for which invention Manby was rewarded by government'.

23 Mathew Carey, *Autobiography* (New York, 1942), p. 9.

24 John Carey, *Learning better than House and Land, as exemplified in the History of Harry Johnson and Dick Hobson* (London: William Darton, n.d. [1824?]), pp 133–4.

see established in the British Empire', and praised 'that undiscriminating spirit of universal toleration' that characterised 'the American Union, where there exists no established state religion'.[25]

Carey's tale of leaving the Old World for the New, like his praise of American meritocracy and religious toleration, means that although *Learning better than House and Land* is not set in Ireland, the story is best read as an emigration narrative, sympathetic to contemporary demands for Catholic emancipation. While critics of the first edition simply regarded the work as a didactive moral tale for children, the additions made by Carey in subsequent editions suggest that he was consciously addressing a dual audience of young and older readers, some of whom he hoped to alert to the political dimensions of his novel. Younger or naive readers of any age could enjoy following the contrasting experiences of Dick Hobson and Harry Johnson, while imbibing the conventional moral message that early application to one's studies leads to success in later life. Certainly, the six illustrations, three of which name Charles Knight (*c.*1742–*c.*1826) as the artist, that appeared in the first three editions supported that straightforward reading. These illustrations, variously depicting the two boys at their lessons (pp 32, 49), the burial of Mrs Johnson (p. 47), the capture of a shark (p. 56), Dick's first meeting with his employer (p. 62), and Harry's ignominious employment as a barber (p. 71), also provided visual detail that enhanced the interest of the text. So, for example, readers could contrast the frugal surroundings of the Hobson hearth where diligent Dick is shown studying at the table with the plush surroundings of the room, complete with elegant drapes and a well-stocked bookcase, where Harry Johnson ignores his lessons and directs his attention to a small dog gambolling on the patterned carpet (p. 32). That contrast is reversed in the final illustration (p. 71) where Harry, now a humble and obsequious barber, is shown bowing before, and accepting a coin from, prosperous Dick. By contrast, the footnotes advocating religious toleration that Carey added to later editions of his novel direct attention away from the text onto broader ethical and social issues. The tone, language and content of these additions suggest that they were addressed not to naive young readers but to parents and tutors involved with the education of the young and therefore likely to read texts primarily intended for their charges. By explicitly attacking religious bigotry in footnotes that displayed a detailed knowledge of recent American history, the editor of Washington's official correspondence deliberately sought to influence political opinion. Building on the critical and commercial success of the first edition of *Learning better than House and Land*, then, John Carey sought in subsequent editions to educate both child and adult readers.

25 John Carey, *Learning better than House and Land, as exemplified in the History of Harry Johnson and Dick Hobson* (London, 1813), p. 133; John Carey, *Learning better than House and Land: as exemplified in the History of Harry Johnson and Dick Hobson* (London, n.d.[1824]), p. 134; see also below, 'Notes', pp 178–9).

By contrast, *Stories of Old Daniel* eschews historical detail in its attempt to enlarge the imaginative experience of young readers. Nevertheless, just as Carey's Irish background provides an enriching context for an appreciation of his fiction, the early experiences of Margaret King Moore, Lady Mount Cashell (1772–1835), inform this pioneering collection of children's stories, notable for its warm portrayal of an unusual adult mentor and his accounts of travel abroad. The eldest daughter and second of twelve children born to Robert King, Viscount Kingsborough of Mitchelstown Castle, Co. Cork, and his wife Caroline, Lady Mount Cashell later recalled: 'being born in that rank of life in which people are too much occupied by frivolous amusements to pay much attention to their offspring I was placed under the care of hirelings from the first moment of my birth', and her childhood was not a happy one, not least because her parents disapproved of her intellectual curiosity.[26] The arrival of a new governess in Mitchelstown in 1786, however, proved an important turning point in the life of young Margaret King, who blossomed under the care of this 'enthusiastic female' who corrected her faults and cultivated her understanding.[27] The governess was Mary Wollstonecraft (1759–97), and although she was dismissed from her position in 1787, she and Margaret corresponded after Wollstonecraft returned to England. There, she drew on her experience in the King household when writing *Original Stories from Real Life* (1788), a work of fiction for young readers in which a mature woman, Mrs Mason, educates two young girls, 'the children of wealthy parents, [who] were, in their infancy, left to the management of servants, or people equally ignorant'.[28] In 1791 Margaret King married Stephen Moore, the earl of Mount Cashell, whom she later described as 'a man whose character was perfectly opposite to mine', but to whom she bore five children within ten years.[29] As a republican and friend of Lord Edward FitzGerald, Lady Mount Cashell supported the cause of the United Irishmen, in defiance of her family's political allegiances. By contrast, her eldest brother, George King, colonel of the North Cork Militia, became renowned for the brutality with which he oversaw the execution and torture of prisoners during the United Irishmen rebellion of 1798. Following the failure of that rebellion, Lady Mount Cashell authored three pamphlets opposing union between Britain and Ireland.[30] When William Godwin, the widower of Mary Wollstonecraft, visited Dublin in July 1800 at the invitation of the liberal politician, John Philpot

26 Edward McAleer, *The Sensitive Plant: A Life of Lady Mount Cashell* (Chapel Hill, NC: University of North Carolina Press, 1958), p. 4.
27 Ibid., p. 5.
28 Mary Wollstonecraft, *Original Stories from Real Life* (London, 1788), p. xi.
29 McAleer, *The Sensitive Plant*, p. 5.
30 For a discussion of the significance of these pamphlets and of Wollstonecraft's influence on Lady Mount Cashell's political thought, see Janet Todd, 'Ascendancy: Lady Mount Cashell, Lady Moira, Mary Wollstonecraft and the Union pamphlets', *Eighteenth-Century Ireland: Iris an dá chultúr*, 18 (2003), 98–117.

Curran, he was introduced to Lady Mount Cashell and they dined together on several occasions in the period following the Acts of Union.[31] On Godwin's return to England, the two corresponded regularly on topics including the baneful effects of tyranny on young minds and the education of children.[32]

Accompanied by her husband, their daughters, and a female companion named Katherine Wilmot, Lady Mount Cashell embarked on a continental tour in 1801. Her first major stop was in London, where she called several times on Godwin in the period preceding his marriage to Mary Jane Clairmont on 21 December 1801. From there, the Mount Cashell party travelled to France and on to Italy. In Rome in 1804, Lady Mount Cashell began a relationship with an Irishman named George William Tighe, and in 1805, separated from the earl, who retained custody of their children. Ostracised by polite society during a period in which she later described herself as 'a vagabond upon the face of the earth', she adopted the pseudonym of 'Mrs Mason', and roamed Europe with Tighe before eventually settling in Pisa.[33] In the closing months of 1807 though, she was in London, where she frequently dined with Godwin,[34] who, with his second wife, had established the Juvenile Library in Hanway Street, London, in 1805. Because of Godwin's association with radical politics, they deemed it prudent not to draw attention to his involvement in a venture dedicated to the publication of children's books, so initially registered the firm in the name of their shop manager, Thomas Hodgkins. Hodgkins was later dismissed for stealing from the till, and, following a move to 41 Skinner Street, Snow Hill, Holborn, in 1807, the firm was re-registered in the name of Mary Jane (M.J.) Godwin.[35] William Godwin, however, was the driving force behind the Juvenile Library's production of progressive children's books, such as his own *Fables Ancient and Modern. Adapted for the Use of Children from Three to Eight Years of Age* (1805), published under the pseudonym of Edward Baldwin, Esq., and Charles and Mary Lamb's *Tales from Shakespear* (1807). Godwin's journal entry for 30 December 1807, which reads: 'Old Daniel published', points to his involvement in the publication of what would prove to be a hugely popular collection of children's stories.[36]

Readers of the first edition of *Stories of Old Daniel; or, Tales of Wonder and Delight*, dated 1808, were not made aware of the identity of the author. Her

31 The Union with Ireland Act 1800 (1800 c.67 39 and 40 Geo 3) was passed on 2 July 1800; the Act of Union (Ireland) 1800 (1800 c.38 40 Geo 3) was passed on 1 August 1800.

32 McAleer, *The Sensitive Plant*, p. 66.

33 Ibid. p. 119.   34 Ibid., p. 121.

35 For more details on Godwin's involvement with the trade in children's books, see Pamela Clemit, 'Philosophical Anarchism in the Schoolroom: William Godwin's Juvenile Library, 1805–25', *Biblion*, 9:1/2 (2000–1), 44–70; Pamela Clemit, 'William Godwin's Juvenile Library', *Charles Lamb Bulletin*, NS 147 (2009), 90–132; Janet Bottoms, 'The Battle of the (Children's) Books', *Romanticism*, 12:3 (2006), 212–22; Janet Bottoms, '"Awakening the mind": the educational philosophy of William Godwin', *History of Education*, 33:3 (2004), 267–82.

36 McAleer, *The Sensitive Plant*, p. 121.

name did not appear on any of the seven subsequent editions of the collection that appeared before the Juvenile Library folded in 1822, or on the sequel, *Continuation of the Stories of Old Daniel* (1820), with the result that both volumes were sometimes attributed to Charles Lamb.[37] Indeed, it was not until 1958 that Edward McAleer established beyond doubt that Lady Mount Cashell drew on recollections of her early life in Ireland and later travels abroad when composing *Stories of Old Daniel*.[38] Written, as she explained in the Preface, 'to indulge that love of the wonderful so natural to children of all ages and dispositions' (p. 79), the volume aimed to turn the thoughts of its young readers 'to foreign countries, and thus induce them to profit by the many well-written books of travels we possess' (p. 79). These objectives were highly unusual for their time, and the introduction of a subtitle, 'narratives of foreign countries and manners' on the second edition (1810) points to the distinctiveness of the volume. In 1801, Maria Edgeworth advised that boys should not read stories about foreign travel unless they were intended for a seafaring life, or for the army, as 'the taste for adventure is absolutely incompatible with the sober perseverance necessary to succeed in any other liberal professions'.[39] *Stories of Old Daniel*, however, shows that a taste for adventure is not necessarily incompatible with the inculcation of moral principles, including sober perseverance.

The collection opens with an introductory chapter that presents the eponymous old Daniel, a retired soldier who lives in an English village, where on Sunday afternoons he treats a group of young boys, including the now adult narrator, to fruit from his garden and tales of his adventures overseas. The following fourteen chapters consist of ten of these stories, which warn against common failings, such as procrastination, unkindness, and dishonesty, but the old man's accounts of his thrilling adventures ensure that his moral instruction indulges his young listeners' love of the wonderful. One tale, 'The Passing of the Pyrenean Mountains', designed to display the desirability of taking advice from those who know more than oneself, describes how Daniel and his companions narrowly escaped two marauding bears while sheltering in a shepherd's hut, close to the border between France and Spain. At the close of the story, the boys make no comment on its moral message but instead ask their 'old friend a number of questions about those ugly animals' and also enquire 'about the construction of the hut' (p. 121), with a view to building a similar one themselves. The narrator recalls: 'I dreamt of the bears that night, and thought I fought most valiantly with one of them' (p. 121). He also recollects that he was so taken with another story in which Daniel's honesty impressed a band of cut-throat thieves that 'all

37 For the attribution to Lamb, see Judith St John, *The Osborne Collection of early Children's Books: a Catalogue*, 2 vols (Toronto: Toronto Public Library, 1958–75), ii, p. 915.
38 McAleer, *The Sensitive Plant*, p. 122.
39 Maria and R.L. Edgeworth, *Practical Education*, in Marilyn Butler (gen ed.), Susan Manly (ed.), *The Works of Maria Edgeworth*, 12 vols (London: Pickering & Chatto, 1993–2003), xi, p. 189.

night I dreamt of the robbers' castle' (p. 91). The ways in which thrilling elements of Old Daniel's improving but adventurous tales invade the narrator's subconscious imagination suggest that Lady Mount Cashell shared Godwin's belief
that 'without imagination there can be no genuine morality'.[40]

One contemporary reviewer objected to Daniel's telling his stories on
Sunday, claiming that this was 'a sly innuendo, not intended to promote the *religious* observance of that sacred day'.[41] Another critic observed: 'we do not
entirely agree with the author in an unrestrained indulgence of that love of the
wonderful so natural to children'.[42] Other commentators reacted more
favourably, variously noting that the volume would 'make an agreeable addition
to the Christmas presents for young people of either sex'; that 'the stories are
sufficiently interesting, and the moral of them is easily comprehended'; and that
Old Daniel 'will be no common favourite with our young friends'.[43] The last
prediction proved accurate, as the fourteenth edition of *Stories of Old Daniel* was
published as late as 1868. Additionally, a new and improved, undated edition,
containing an extra story, 'The Roman Beggar', appeared under the imprint of
M.J. Godwin at the premises in Skinner Street, from which the firm moved in
1822. This edition contained some variations to the text of the stories that had
appeared in the original 1808 edition, notably in the form of simplification of
phraseology and vocabulary to render them more accessible to young readers.
For example, Old Daniel's beard was of the same 'color' rather than 'hue' (p. 83)
of his hair; the children 'loved' instead of 'doated on' (p. 83) him; and he was
always 'followed' rather than 'accompanied' (p. 83) by a dog.[44] Despite the mis-
givings of some critics, *Stories of Old Daniel* sufficiently captivated its young readers to warrant its reissue both in its original and amended forms.

A great deal of the collection's appeal undoubtedly lay in the removal of the
action from the domestic settings favoured by other writers of early children's
fiction. In 'Dog Trusty's Ancestor', Lady Mount Cashell invoked Maria
Edgeworth's tale of 'Little Dog Trusty', a story that appeared in *The Parent's
Assistant* (1796), as well as in *Early Lessons* (1801). Subtitled 'The liar and the boy
of truth', Edgeworth's story introduces two young brothers, honest Frank and
deceitful Robert, who overturn a basin of milk intended for supper. Robert
blames the mishap on Trusty, the little dog who has been sleeping by the fire, but
Frank tells the truth and so saves Trusty from being beaten by their mother.
Instead, Robert is soundly whipped by his father, while Frank, in recognition of

---

40 Cited in C. Kegan Paul, *William Godwin, His Friends and Contemporaries*, 2 vols (London,
    1876), ii, p. 119.
41 *The Literary Panorama* (November 1808), 272.
42 *The London Review and Literary Journal* (April 1808), 289.
43 *British Critic*, 33 (1809), 78; *Monthly Review* (April 1809), 430; *The Critical Review; or, Annals of
    Literature*, Third Series, 14:1 (May 1808), 110.
44 *Stories of Old Daniel; or, Tales of Wonder and Delight*, A new and Improved Edition (London,
    n.d,), pp 1, 2.

his truthfulness, becomes sole owner of Trusty. The entire drama unfolds within a domestic setting in which parental authority reigns supreme. By contrast, 'Dog Trusty's Ancestor' eschews the domestic in favour of adventure abroad. At Grotto del Cane in Naples, Daniel and his friend rescue a dog who is about to be sent into a cave to demonstrate the effects of the poisonous gas that circulates within. The dog later foils an assault on his rescuers and lives out his days as the faithful companion of Daniel's kindly friend. Trusty, the dog owned by Daniel and beloved of the village boys, is the descendant of that loyal canine hero. The story's non-domestic setting precludes a conventional endorsement of parental authority and instead allows for the telling of a thrilling adventure story that nonetheless illustrates the necessity 'always to treat brutes with the greatest humanity' (p. 126). 'Dog Trusty's Ancestor' shares a Neapolitan setting with 'The Little Merchants', a story which Edgeworth introduced in the third edition of *The Parent's Assistant* (1800). 'The Little Merchants' contrasts young Francisco, who is reared by his parents to be honest with the result that the family prosper, and Piedro, a boy who comes to a predictably bad end because his father teaches him to be sharp and cunning. Essentially, Edgeworth provides an incidental foreign background to a conventional domestic tale that stresses the importance of parental example on developing minds. Old Daniel's story, by contrast, avoids all mention of parents and children, instead featuring an entirely adult cast that includes himself and his former commanding officer, a mercenary Neapolitan dog-owner, a postillion of dubious honesty, a villainous inn-keeper and his treacherous sons. As a result, 'Dog Trusty's Ancestor' is both exotic and exciting.

Here, and throughout the volume, authority is not invested in parents, or even a teacher, but in an uneducated old man whom children love, respect, and occasionally fear. The frontispiece to the 1808 edition (p. 76), which has been attributed to William Blake, captures the intensity of that relationship.[45] In it, Old Daniel is shown sitting in a wicker chair outside his door, brandishing a stick in his left hand while resting his right hand on the back of one of a group of five boys sitting and kneeling around him in rapt attention. Susan, the old man's daughter, stands behind him, a cat and dog sit at his feet, and a cage containing a starling hangs from the wall of the cottage. The frontispiece by Henry Corbould (1787–1844) that appeared in subsequent editions [2] respects the essential elements of the original composition but introduces some changes that affect the depiction of the relationship between the old man and his audience. In Corbould's illustration, Old Daniel looks stern but while his left arm is still raised, the stick rests at the side of his chair so that he appears less threatening, while his dog turns from a faintly menacing mastiff into a decidedly sentimentalized collie. Only four young boys kneel before him while four older youths,

---

45 The attribution to Blake is made in a handwritten, unsigned and undated note in the seventh edition of *Stories of Old Daniel* (London, 1820), held by the Victoria and Albert Museum (60.B.64).

one barely visible, stand behind them so that the sense of intimacy is less pronounced than in the original. In both, however, the boys' attention is focused on the old man, rendering his influence over them clearly visible.

Old Daniel imaginatively transports his audience, who vicariously share his adventures, from a sedate English setting to locations as varied as the north of Ireland, France, Spain, Germany, and Italy. Given that the volume was first published during the Napoleonic Wars, the old man's stories of camaraderie, bravery and adventure could be perceived as subtle recruitment aids, but it is telling that the horrors of the battlefield are acknowledged and condemned. Because Lady Mount Cashell draws on her own experiences and is vague, sometimes contradictory, about chronology, it is difficult to date Daniel's military career or subsequent exploits with any precision. The narrator recalls first meeting the old man some forty years ago (p. 85) during the summer in which Daniel celebrated his ninety-fourth birthday (p. 122). Given that *Stories of Old Daniel* appeared in the first decade of the nineteenth century and that Daniel could only have been in his early twenties at most when he 'was a very young lad, and first went into the army' (p. 88), he must have been a soldier around the turn of the seventeenth and eighteenth centuries and could have participated in the War of the Spanish Succession (1701–14). However, the references to 'the dreadful accidents of civil war' (p. 127) and the 'horrible sights ... that follow after a battle' (p. 129) seem to draw more on Lady Mount Cashell's knowledge of the atrocities of the 1798 rebellion than on any identifiable European conflict. The lack of precision does not detract from the stories, though, because they are less concerned with providing realistic accounts of warfare than with awakening children's imaginations to the wonders of travel, 'without distorting their young minds by any thing too horrible or unnatural' (p. 79) .

Despite this acknowledged avoidance of the unpleasant, the stories include some disturbing, even gruesome, elements. Part of the action of 'The Church-Yard' takes place in an eerie graveyard where 'the ground was strewed with skulls which were whitened by the air' (p. 85). The story is told 'for the purpose of correcting a little boy ... who had been taught by a foolish maid-servant to be afraid of ghosts' (p. 87), but it operates on the very dynamic of terror that it ostensibly condemns. 'The Man-Hater', which extends over three chapters, is equally disconcerting. The central character is a hermit named Henry, raised near Leghorn, who entrusts a manuscript to Old Daniel and his travelling companion in the hope that others will hear the story of his misspent life. Before he saw the error of his ways, the selfishness of this eldest son of indulgent parents resulted in the deaths of his younger brother, Felix, and his best friend, who loved him dearly. Henry becomes enamoured of the beautiful daughter of a friend of his father, a rich merchant who has fallen on hard times. Henry fails both of them, with the result that the merchant dies and his daughter is left destitute. This accumulation of misfortune, brought about by his own self-absorption, disturbs the balance of Henry's mind, and he removes himself to a German forest, 'remote from the haunts of men' (p. 140). Elements of this disturbing narrative recur in *Frankenstein; or, The Modern Prometheus* (1808), suggesting that Old Daniel's story lingered in the subconscious imagination of Mary Godwin Shelley, who was living with her father when Lady Mount Cashell regularly visited him in 1807 prior to the publication *Stories of Old Daniel*. Given both this contact and the early connection between Lady Mount Cashell and Mary Wollstonecraft, it seems fitting that Mary Shelley's gothic tale of a motherless creature should have close affinities with a disturbing story for children written by her deceased mother's favourite Irish pupil.

An equally intriguing continuum between adult literature and children's fiction is exemplified by the publication history of a fable which first appeared in the opening volume of *The Fool of Quality; or, The History of Henry, Earl of Moreland*, written by Henry Brooke (1703–83), and published 'for the autor [sic]' in Dublin in 1765. The son of a wealthy rector, Brooke studied at Trinity College Dublin and at the Temple in London before practising as a chamber counsel in Dublin. A long religious poem, *Universal Beauty* (1735), established his reputation as a writer, leading him to abandon the law and move to London to establish a career as a dramatist. There, his play, *Gustavus Vasa* (1739), loosely based on the career of the hero who liberated Sweden from Danish rule, was seen as a critique of Sir Robert Walpole, and became the first work to be banned following the theatre licensing act of 1737. Brooke returned to Ireland, where he interested himself in antiquarian pursuits and political controversies. In a series of *Farmer's Letters* (1745–60), he moved from attacking Catholicism, because of its links with Jacobitism, to arguing that the Penal Laws were against Protestant interests, while in *The Tryal of the Cause of the Roman Catholics* (1761), he argued for a relaxation of those laws. Brooke's best-known literary work was *The Fool of Quality, or, The History of Henry Earl of Moreland*, a five-volume, sentimental novel that reflected his interest in Methodism. Indeed, the novel became such a favourite with Methodists that John Wesley requested permission to improve it. As Brooke was ill, his nephew replied on his behalf, reporting that his uncle cordially embraced Wesley's kind offer, granting him permission '*to prune, erase, and alter*' as he pleased.[46] Wesley's two-volume abridgement appeared under the title *Henry, Earl of Moreland*, in 1781.

The Fool of Quality opens with an entertaining dialogue between the author and reader that reveals the influence on the novel's digressive narrative style of Laurence Sterne's *The Life and Opinions of Tristram Shandy, Gentleman* (1759–67). As *The Fool of Quality* charts the natural upbringing of Harry Moreland, the second son of an English earl, the actual story underlines Brooke's indebtedness to *Émile* (1762), Jean-Jacques Rousseau's treatise on the nature of man and the purpose of education. While an infant, Harry is sent to live with the family of a

---

46 Letter dated 6 August 1774 from Henry Brooke, nephew of the author of *The Fool of Quality*, in *Bookman*, 9:51 (Dec. 1895), p. 81.

neighbouring farmer, with whom he happily remains until he comes to the attention of a benevolent stranger, Mr Fenton, who eventually turns out to be his paternal uncle. This virtuous relative does all in his power to ensure that Harry grows into an exemplary young man, at one point telling him a fable about three silver trout in order to curb the boy's inordinate desire for strength and knowledge. The first little fish longs for wings and ends up dying a gruesome death when his wish is granted; the second, who discovers the dangers of venturing from home, expires from a surfeit of care and anxiety, while the third humbly accepts whatever God thinks is best for him. Mr Fenton leaves Harry 'to ruminate on what he had heard' (p. 150), instead of interpreting a fable whose sentiments have much in common with the opening lines of John Wesley's Covenant Prayer: 'I am no longer my own, but yours. Put me to what you will'.[47] The following day, Harry begins to guess at its meaning, suggesting that, like the third little fish, he should leave everything to God. Mr Fenton readily confirms this interpretation, but is taken aback when the boy expresses sympathy for 'the two poor little naughty Trouts' (p. 150) and wonders why a loving God should 'make any Thing to dye' (p. 150). Mr Fenton tells him that he thinks too deeply and defers discussion of this theological dilemma to another time. In its original presentation, then, the fable of the little fishes, designed to foster the ethical development of a wilful, impressionable boy, unexpectedly reveals that the child is capable of a type of profound deliberation that points towards the superficiality of conventional moral instruction.

Brooke's fable, which first appeared in a novel addressed to adults, took on a life of its own, being adapted in many and various forms, reflecting different levels of didactic intent, in a wide range of texts addressed specifically to children well into the nineteenth century.[48] For Samuel Johnson, a fable was, 'in its genuine state a narrative in which beings irrational, and sometimes inanimate ... are for the purpose of moral instruction, feigned to act and speak with human interests and passions'.[49] Johnson's association of 'moral instruction' with this type of

47 Frank Whaling (ed.), *John and Charles Wesley: Selected Prayers, Hymns, Journal Notes, Sermons, Letters and Treaties* (London: SPCK; New York: Paulist Press, 1981), p. 387.

48 In addition to the two versions reproduced in this volume, these texts included Anon, *The History of Three Silver Trouts: Decorated with Cuts* (London, 1820); Edward Payson, *The Pastor's Daughter* (London, 1835), pp 21–3; Rev. D. Newell (ed.), *The Christian Family Magazine; or, Parents' and Children's Annual*, Vol. 1 (New York; Philadelphia; Boston, 1842), p. 25; *The Workingman's Friend and Family Instructor* (Saturday 16 October 1852), 34; E.T. Stevens and Charles Hole, *The Complete Reader: Being a Carefully Graduated System of Teaching to Read and Spell by Means of Attractive and Instructive Lessons. In Four Books, especially Designed for Upper and Middle-class Schools. Book II – The Intermediate Reader* (London: Longmans, Green, and Co., 1866), pp 17–18. Similarly, Sarah Fielding, in *The Governess; or, Little Female Academy* (London, 1749), pp 233–6, reproduced extracts from Brooke's poem, 'The sparrow and the dove', which first appeared in Edward Moore's *Fables for the Female Sex* (London, 1744), pp 89–113.

49 Samuel Johnson, 'Gay', *The Lives of the English Poets; and a Criticism on their Works*, 3 vols (London, 1779–81), iii, p. 14.

tale highlights its suitability for use in the education of the young, and indeed it has been claimed that fables written on cuneiform tablets were used in class-rooms in what is now Iran and Iraq as early as two thousand years BCE.[50] In eighteenth-century Europe, however, opinion was divided on the effect of fables on young minds. John Locke, for example, described Aesop's fables as 'stories apt to delight and entertain a child' but Jean-Jacques Rousseau argued that children should not be told such stories because, incapable of understanding their allegorical meaning, they interpret them 'in a manner contrary to the intention of the fabulist'.[51] Harry Moreland's reaction to Mr Fenton's story of the three fishes shows that it can indeed be difficult to predict a child's response to a fable. To circumvent that difficulty, instead of allowing children to decode the allegory and work out the meaning for themselves, as Mr Fenton did with Harry, authors, from Aesop onwards, often drew attention to the intended moral. The full title of Sarah Trimmer's *Fabulous Histories. Designed for the Instruction of Children, respecting their Treatment of Animals* (1786), for instance, guided readers' interpretation of a text that told the parallel stories of two families, one of humans and the other of robins. In the introduction, Trimmer explained that children should not suppose that birds can really speak but should instead read the avian conversations, which 'recommend *universal Benevolence*', as 'a series of Fables, intended to convey moral instruction to themselves'.[52] In similar fashion, adaptors of Brooke's fable of the three little fishes frequently took care to present an unambiguous moral message to young readers.

That is certainly the case in the version that appeared in the anonymously authored *The History of Master Billy Friendly, and his Sister Miss Polly Friendly: to which is added, the Fairy Tale of the Three Little Fishes* (*c*.1787). The volume opens with an introductory message in which young readers are advised to 'Fear God, honour your parents, love your brothers and sisters, behave politely to your friends, and learn your books'.[53] 'The History of Master Billy Friendly', the first story which follows this opening address, shows how advantageous it can be to follow such advice. Billy begins life as a good little boy whose mother rewards his diligence at lessons by presenting him with a pretty dog. He never misses church, says prayers every morning and evening, and is so eager to get to school that his father gives him a little horse. When he grows up, God repays his virtue by blessing him to such an extent that he is elected to parliament, rides in a fine

50 See Gillian Adams, 'Ancient and medieval children's texts', in Peter Hunt (ed.), *International Encyclopedia of Children's Literature*, 2 vols (London: Routledge, 2004), i, pp 225–38, p. 226.

51 John Locke, *Some Thoughts concerning Education* (London: A. & J. Churchill, 1693), pp 183–4; Jean-Jacques Rousseau, *Emilius and Sophia; or, A new system of education*, 2 vols (London: R. Griffiths, 1762), i, p. 192.

52 Mrs Trimmer, *Fabulous Histories. Designed for the Instruction of Children, respecting their Treatment of Animals* (London, 1786), pp x–xi.

53 Anon., *The History of Master Billy Friendly, and his Sister Miss Polly Friendly: to which is added, the Fairy Tale of the Three Little Fishes* (London, n.d. [*c*.1787]), p. 2.

chariot, and becomes a very rich man, whose own son 'exactly copies his papa'.[54] The second story, 'The History of Miss Polly Friendly' presents Billy's sister, who leads an equally virtuous and charmed existence, largely because she follows her brother's example. When Polly owns up to breaking some of the family's fine china, her mother presents her with a robin and a watch. Her graceful dancing and her progress at the harpsichord delight both her parents, while her kindness to the poor impresses 'Mr Alderman *Foresight*, who was always of opinion, that virtue and industry were the best portion with a wife'.[55] The two marry, and Polly soon becomes a finely dressed lady, who 'rides in the fine gilt coach drawn by prancing horses'.[56] Commenting on the 'model of socio-economic advancement through literacy and good behaviour' that under-pins the presentation of the Friendly paragons, Andrew O'Malley noted: 'we … begin to see here an acknowledgment of a middle-class domestic ideology and a differentiation of social virtue by gender'.[57] While this observation is undoubt-edly true of the first two stories that make up the volume, it is less applicable to the third, an adaptation of Brooke's fable entitled 'A Curious and Instructive Tale of Three Little Fishes'. In contrast to the model of social advancement through literacy and responsible conduct that shapes the histories of both Billy and Polly Friendly, this version of the tale of the little fishes advocates contented acceptance of one's station in life.

Here, without any acknowledgment of Brooke, his fable is recast as a fairy tale, to which is appended an 'Application', which clearly sets out the correct moral interpretation for young readers. While fairy tales are often about characters who get what they want against all the odds and are happy with the outcome, fables tend to feature characters who, as Perry Nodelman observed, 'are wrong to want what they want and learn their error by getting what they desire'.[58] In this version of Brooke's fable, the emphasis is very much on correcting error and denouncing desire. As in the original, the story concerns three little fishes, two of whom become discontented with their situation. Instead of God, though, a fairy undertakes to grant their wishes, touching the first with her wand so that he sprouts wings and travels far before dying, like his predecessor, of starvation. The second fish wants to be changed into a mouse. The fairy grants his wish, whereupon he rushes to a pantry where he is taken, killed and eaten by a cat. The third little fish, prudently learning from the experience of the others, says his only desire is that the fairy will do with him what she will, so she leaves him as he is, allowing him to live happily ever after. Perhaps because some contemporary commentators, including Sarah Trimmer, believed that fairy tales encouraged irrational, superstitious beliefs and so had a

---

54 Ibid., p. 17.   55 Ibid., p. 33.   56 Ibid., pp 34–5.

57 Andrew O'Malley, *The Making of the Modern Child: Children's Literature and Childhood in the late Eighteenth Century* (London: Routledge, 2003), p. 31.

58 Perry Nodelman, *The Hidden Adult* (Baltimore: Johns Hopkins University Press, 2008), p. 81.

pernicious effect on young minds, the benevolent primacy of a Christian God is carefully asserted in the 'Application' that follows: 'Children should learn betimes to fear God, and to serve him rightly, and he will give them all that is proper for them, as he best knows what is for their good' (p. 154). In its original presentation, the story was designed to curb Harry Moreland's inordinate desire for strength and knowledge, so that the first little fish longs for the speed and agility of a bird while the second wants to understand the meaning of events he has witnessed. Here, by contrast, the story is adapted to highlight the perceived virtues of humility and self-denial, so that the two dissatisfied, proud fishes who meet bad ends are portrayed as deserving their misfortune. The allegorical meaning of the fable is limited to the unequivocal message that 'if people were to be indulged in all their desires, they would bring nothing but distress, and ruin on themselves' (p. 154). Unlike Harry Moreland, readers of 'A Curious and Instructive Tale of Three Little Fishes' are not encouraged to make sense of the story themselves or allowed to ponder the moral ambiguities that it, perhaps unintentionally, suggests.

The interpretative possibilities of the fable are similarly limited in the version that John Clowes (1743–1831) presented to child readers and to adults charged with the religious education of the young in 1801. The author of this instructional tract was a Church of England clergyman who worked as a private tutor until ill-health precluded his continuance with that profession, leading him to accept the rectorship of St John's, Manchester in 1769. An admirer of Emmanuel Swedenborg (1688–1722), who believed that the Divine Trinity existed in the person of Jesus Christ, Clowes translated five of the Swedish philosopher's works into English, beginning with the *Vera Christiana Religio* (1781). In 1782, he founded a Society of Gentlemen in Manchester with a view to printing and circulating Swedenborg's teachings and his own elucidations of them. Despite some pressure to consider his role as an Anglican minister, he retained his position as rector of St John's for over fifty years, during which time he 'took an active part in the Sunday-schools and was himself a diligent teacher'.[59] So diligent was he that his congregation erected a plaque 'to mark their gratitude for his labours of love in the promotion of Sunday Schools, and in the moral and religious education of the young'.[60] On the occasion of his funeral in St John's, it was reported that 'the Sunday School children were ranged in line from the door to the gates'.[61] His obituarist noted that in addition to his translations and elucidations of Swedenborg, Clowes 'published at different times many other works connected with religion'.[62] One of these works, published by the Society of Gentlemen, was *The Three Little Fishes, a*

59 Theodore Compton, *The life and correspondence of the Reverend John Clowes, M.A.: formerly fellow of Trinity College, Cambridge, and rector for sixty-two years of St. John's, Manchester* (London, 1882), p. 28.

60 Ibid., p. 91.

61 *The Gentleman's Magazine*, 101 (July 1831), 89.

62 Ibid., 88.

Story, intended for the Instruction of Youth: together with an Exhortation to the Right Observance of the Sabbath Day, and a Discourse on the Benefit of Sunday Schools. Selected from the History of Harry Moreland.[63]

The first part of this tract introduces Harry Moreland as a fine boy, beloved by his parents, who unfortunately began to 'manifest symptoms of discontent in his low station in life, and expressed frequent wishes, in the presence of his parents, that he had been born to a better station' (p. 158). His father, wishing to curb this tendency in his son, tells him the story of the three little fishes, exactly as it appeared in *The Fool of Quality*. Harry's reaction to the story, 'intended to make him content and thankful to GOD' (p. 161), is described in the opening of the second part of the tract, which proceeds to recount how his father's exhortations to keep holy the Sabbath day prove equally efficacious. The text of these exhortations, minus the opening paragraph in which Harry provides the link between sections, appeared anonymously as Tract 14 in the first volume of *The Publications of the Religious Tract Society*, also published in 1801. The final section describes how Harry's concerned father addresses a neighbouring family, who are lax about the religious education of the younger members, impressing on them the spiritual and temporal benefits that accrue from attendance at Sunday School. A closing note reads: '*Any well-wisher to Parents who cannot read this Address, is requested to read it to them*' (p. 167). Here, then, Brooke's story of the fishes is incorporated into an instructional tract addressed to children and adults alike. Although Clowes faithfully follows the wording of the original fable, the context in which it is presented guides and limits the interpretation of readers of all ages.

While commentators disagree on what exactly distinguishes children's fiction from writing addressed to more mature readers, the prevailing critical consensus is that the two are qualitatively different. When discussing the distinctive features of children's fiction, critics usually refer to its simplicity of diction, its brevity, its focus on childhood experience, its focalization through a child or childlike char-

63 Clowes's other publications for young readers included *The Pastor's New Year's Gift to his Little Flock, teaching them how to serve God, etc.* (Manchester, 1796); *The Caterpillars and the Gooseberry Bush* (Manchester, 1800); *The mysterious Ladder; or, Jacob's Dream interpreted and explained. In two Dialogues between a Father and his Son. Designed for the Instruction of Youth* (Manchester, 1810); *The Rainbow; or, The Token of God's Covenant with his People. In two Dialogues between a Father and his Son. Designed for the Instruction of Youth* (Manchester, 1810); *The Young Prince: an Allegory: Shewing how he set out to return to his Father's Kingdom, and of what befel him in the way, and of the glorious things which he saw and heard in his Father's Kingdom*, 5th ed. (Manchester, 1810); *The Golden Wedding Ring, or, Thoughts on Marriage in a Conversation between a Father and his two Children* (Manchester, 1813); *An Explanation of the Church Catechism, for the Use of Young People*, 4th ed. (Manchester, 1818).

64 See, for example, Judith Hillman, *Discovering Children's Literature*, 2nd ed. (Upper Saddle River, New Jersey: Merrill, 1999), p. 3; Myles McDowell, 'Fiction for children and adults: some essential differences', *Children's Literature in Education*, 4:1 (1973), 50–63, p. 51; Fred Inglis, *The Promise of Happiness: Value and Meaning in Children's Fiction* (Cambridge: Cambridge

acter, its concentration on dialogue and action, and its mode of narration.[64] Following Jacqueline Rose's influential flagging of 'the impossibility of children's fiction', critics increasingly recognize that the binary opposition between child and adult, and the unequal power relationship underpinning that conceptual opposition, are central to the dynamics of that form of writing.[65] The common motivation behind all the stories included in this volume was undoubtedly the desire of adult writers to influence child readers, encouraging them to become particular types of adults themselves. These stories therefore suggest that one distinguishing characteristic of early children's fiction was its reflection of the conviction that adult writers could, and should, shape the moral development of children. Implicit in this conviction are an endorsement of the ideological power of fiction and a subtle repudiation of parental authority: Harry Moreland ponders a fable that he hears from Mr Fenton; Dick Hobson is inspired by the story that he reads of Dick Whittington; the village boys delight in hearing Old Daniel's tales of adventure. Defined by a readership that by virtue of its youth is invariably subject to adult control, children's fiction asserts an influence over its audience that may appear to complement, but actually supersedes, parental authority.

The historian, Thomas Bartlett, has argued that the profoundly unequal parent-child paradigm is the most appropriate description of eighteenth-century Anglo-Irish relations.[66] That argument is supported by varying recourse to the parent-child analogy in the political discourse of the later period. An anonymous Irish critic of English policy in Ireland, for example, claimed in 1772: 'We have been treated, of late, not as the children, but the bastards of our mother country; and all our expectations of an equal distribution of inheritance are considered, not as claims of right, but as pretences of contumacy, and presumption'.[67] Some years later, by contrast, a supporter of union with England contended: 'Were the thoughts of England hostile and designing, she would not present this union. She would say to her colony ... you have been a bad child, and I disinherit you. This would be the language of the angry parent'.[68] Another commentator similarly commented: 'A Legislative Union with Great Britain is

University Press, 1981), pp 101–2; Nodelman, *The Hidden Adult*, pp 76–81; Barbara Wall, *The Narrator's Voice: the Dilemma of Children's Fiction* (Basingstoke: Macmillan, 1990), pp 2–3.
65 Jacqueline Rose, *The Case of Peter Pan; or, The Impossibility of Children's Fiction* (Basingstoke: Macmillan, 1994); for critics who endorse Rose's position, see Charles Sarland, 'The impossibility of innocence: ideology, politics, and children's literature' in Peter Hunt (ed.), *Understanding Children's Literature: Key Essays from the second edition of The International Companion Encyclopedia of Children's Literature* (London: Routledge, 2005), pp 39–55; Perry Nodelman, *The Hidden Adult*, pp 157–72.
66 Thomas Bartlett, *The Fall and Rise of the Irish Nation: the Catholic Question, 1690–1830* (Dublin: Gill and Macmillan, 1992), pp 36–7.
67 *Baratariana. A select collection of fugitive political pieces, published during the administration of Lord Townshend in Ireland* (Dublin, 1772), p. 2.
68 Thomas Richard Bentley, *Considerations upon the state of public affairs, in the year MDCCXCIX* (London, 1799), pp 85–6.

proposed. The mother country opens out her arms to embrace and relieve the child which had deserted her'.[69] Given this politically charged use of the parent–child relationship, it is significant that *Learning better than House and Land*, *Stories of Old Daniel*, and Henry Brooke's original presentation of the fable of the little fishes all eschew domestic settings and replace parental authority with authorial influence. It is true that Dick Hobson has well-intended, loving parents who do their best for their son, but as his mother is an ignorant peasant and his father's livelihood depends on an absentee landlord, these two humble, exemplary figures, whose orphaned son makes a success of life in America, can be seen as more Irish than English. As a result of their shared displacement of parental authority, the stories included in the present volume implicitly engage with contemporary debates on Anglo–Irish relations. In more general terms, the stories demonstrate that John Carey, Lady Mount Cashell, and Henry Brooke – three Irish writers from diverse social backgrounds, and with disparate political allegiances and religious loyalties – expanded the frontiers of early children's fiction in English. Together, they help stake out a claim for the importance children's fiction might hold for anyone concerned with the literature, Irish or otherwise, of the long eighteenth century.

69 George Cooper, *Letters on the Irish nation: written during a visit to that kingdom, in the autumn of the year 1799* (London, 1800), p. 170.

A note on the texts

The text of John Carey's *Learning better than House and Land, as exemplified in the History of a 'Squire and a Cow-herd* in the present edition follows that of the first edition, published in London by B. Tabart and Co. in 1808, using the Victoria and Albert Museum Library copy (60.T.59).

The volume was reissued by the same firm as *Learning better than House and Land, as exemplified in the History of Harry Johnson and Dick Hobson* in 1810. A third amended and slightly expanded edition, bearing the altered subtitle, was published by W. Darton in 1813, and an undated fourth edition, also bearing the amended subtitle, was subsequently published by the same firm.

Because of the rarity of the first edition, and the delicate condition of those few copies that survive, the illustrations in the present volume are taken from the second edition of 1810, using the Trinity College Dublin copy (OLS B-2-936).

The text of Lady Mount Cashell's *Stories of Old Daniel; or, Tales of Wonder and Delight* follows that of the first edition, published anonymously by the Proprietors of the Juvenile Library in London in 1808, using the British Library copy (Ch.800/51.[1.]). The eighth edition was published by the same firm in 1822. A small number of emendations have been made to copy-text and are listed on p. 186. The frontispiece is taken from the first edition.

The text of Henry Brooke's fable of the fishes is taken from pages 50–9 of the first edition of the first volume of *The Fool of Quality; or, The History of Henry, Earl of Moreland*, published in Dublin in 1765, using the British Library copy (1488.h.6.).

The text of 'A Curious and Instructive Tale of Three Little Fishes' is taken from pages 37–44 of the undated *The History of Master Billy Friendly, and his Sister Miss Polly Friendly: to which is added, the Fairy Tale of the Three Little Fishes*, published anonymously in London by John Marshall, using the University of California Libraries copy (10476603). The approximate date of 1787 was suggested by the Iona and Peter Opie in the catalogue of their collection at the Bodleian Library. One emendation has been made to copy-text and is listed on p. 186.

The text of John Clowes's *The Three Little Fishes, a Story, intended for the Instruction of Youth: together with an Exhortation to the Right Observance of the Sabbath Day, and a Discourse on the Benefit of Sunday Schools. Selected from the History of Harry Moreland* is taken from the only edition, published in Manchester in 1801, using the British Library copy (RB.23.a.33297). A few emendations have been made to copy-text and are listed on p. 186.

Learning better than House and Land

The Education of Mast^r. H. Johnson

From *Learning better than House and Land* (2nd ed.; London, 1810)

LEARNING

BETTER THAN

HOUSE AND LAND,

AS EXEMPLIFIED IN THE

History

OF

A 'SQUIRE AND A COW–HERD.

—◆—

By J. CAREY, LL.D

Private Teacher
of the Classics, French, English and Short-hand.

—◆—

LONDON.

PRINTED FOR B. TABART AND CO.

AT THE JUVENILE LIBRARY, NEW BOND STREET,

By Turner and Harwood, St. John's Square, Clerkenwell.

1808.

Approved, as a teacher, by families of distinguished rank, who have experienced his careful attitude and successful method — the writer of this little history — author like-wise of various other publications, and translator of several works from the French* — would instruct a Youth in the* CLASSICS, *French, English and Short-hand, or visit a respectable Female Seminary, to teach English Grammar, with* COMPOSITION *in Prose and Verse.*

His SHORT-HAND *may separately be learned in four Lessons* — price two Guineas — which he engages to refund on the production of any other system (now publicly known in England) that shall prove superior to his in simplicity, facility, and clearness.*

Letters (post paid) may be addressed to "Dr Carey, Islington."

He has just published a new edition of his "Latin Prosody made easy" with considerable improvements.*

July 16, 1808.*

*An Apology**

may justly be deemed necessary for offering to the public a trifle of this kind, which indeed was not originally written with a view to publication, but solely intended for the amusement and instruction of an amiable and interesting youth, whom I was in the habit of visiting as a private tutor. A friend, however, who happened to see it in manuscript before I presented it to my young pupil,* urged me to print it. In complying with his desire, I am well aware, that, as a literary composition, this little tale has no claim to praise: but, as a lesson to youth, it may perhaps prove useful; and on that utility alone I rest my hope that the parent or instructor of my juvenile reader will pardon its deficiency in other respects. As to the professed periodical critics, I have nothing to fear from them; my humble production lying too far below the range of their artillery, which, like the bolts of Jove* only strikes more exalted objects.

In certain parts of the narrative, which contain facts of some importance to natural history or philosophy, the youthful reader will of course wish to know whether he reads truth or fiction. I therefore assure him beforehand, that he will not, in any one of those passages, find a single material fact related, which is not strictly true. I shall, in another place, make a few remarks on each subject; not choosing here to anticipate.

With respect to trans-atlantic hospitality—in bestowing on it a line of incidental commendation, I have by no means out-stepped the bounds of truth.* On the contrary, the hospitable disposition of the Americans justly merits much higher encomium,* and from a happier pen than mine. It shines most eminently conspicuous in the southern states of the Union, where any decently-dressed man may travel a thousand miles without ever entering an inn. In a tour which I made through a part of that extensive region, although I usually, and for very obvious reasons, preferred to lodge at public inns, yet, on two occasions, I was glad to avail myself of private hospitality.—I shall here briefly notice one of them.

In the western tract of Virginia, beyond the Blue Ridge of the Apalachian mountains, in the month of January, in deep snow, with a violent drifting wind, I lost my way in the woods between Martinsburg and Winchester.*

After long and circuitous wanderings—after having fasted and ridden from breakfast-time till past sun-set—at length, instead of being reduced to sleep under a tree (my last, my long, interminable sleep!) I fortunately arrived, about dark, at the plantation of Ignatius Perry, Esquire. As I approached the house, a negro* came out to take my horse; and, while I was inquiring of him whether his master were at home, a young gentleman, about the age of twelve or thirteen, made his appearance at the door, with Mrs. Perry's compliments, politely inviting me to dismount, and walk in. On my introduction to her, I explained the cause of my unpremeditated visit, and was cordially welcomed.

Though the family had dined some hours before, a hot dinner of four or five dishes, fish, flesh, and fowl, was prepared for me with a degree of expedition, which could hardly have been surpassed, if they had been forewarned of my arrival. To keep me in countenance, covers were laid for Mrs. Perry, her son, and her daughters, who all sat down to table with me, and *pretended* to eat. A smiling bowl of rich apple-toddy†, followed by a glass of excellent Madeira, comfortably diluted my hearty meal; and the agreeable conversation of Mrs. Perry and her daughters—two sensible, pleasing young women, who, in those qualities, perfectly resembled their amiable mother—gave an additional zest to the entertainment.

I was retiring to rest at an early hour, and in the act of wishing the family good night, when in came Mr. Perry, returned from a journey or a visit. He saluted me, not with formal distance, as a stranger dropped from the clouds, but with easy familiarity, as if I had been an old acquaintance. On my repeating to him the cause of my appearance in his parlour, he was "happy that chance, had directed me to *his* house, and hoped, that, in his absence, I had been entertained to my satisfaction."

After some conversation with him, I was now finally retiring for the night, and returning my thanks to the ladies and young gentleman for their hospitality and politeness, "as I should probably not have the pleasure of seeing them in the morning; it being my intention to start at an early hour for Winchester"—but Mr. Perry interrupted me, by observing, that, "when a gentleman did him the favor of sleeping under his roof, he always expected the pleasure of his company at breakfast the next day".

At breakfast, on my expressing a wish that a negro might be ordered to saddle my horse, "'Tis Sunday," said Mr Perry: "you can do no business in town to-day. You shall sleep here to-night: Winchester is only six miles distant; and you can, to-morrow morning, reach it early enough for any business that you may have to transact."

Before breakfast, however, I had learned from Master Perry—an intelligent, good-natured youth, and likely to prove an agreeable fellow-traveler—

† A mixture of rum, water, and sugar, enriched with the soft pulp of roasted apples—with or without nutmeg.

that he was to return on the Sunday evening to the boarding-school at Winchester after the Christmas holidays; in consequence of which information, I made a different arrangement with his father, informing him that I should be glad to take advantage of the young gentleman's guidance, for fear of again losing my way in the woods.

At my departure with him after dinner, Mr. Perry politely "thanked me for the pleasure of my company, and hoped, that, if ever I should again pass through that part of the country, I would favor him with a visit."

Such is Virginian hospitality—with this exception, however, that there was not the smallest necessity for me to stand parleying with the negro at the door. I might at once have commanded him to take my horse—have instantly alighted—walked in without hesitation, and experienced precisely the same reception—a reception, which neither the distance of four thousand miles, nor the revolution of nineteen years,* has yet been able to efface from my grateful remembrance.

J.C*

LEARNING

BETTER THAN

HOUSE AND LAND.

IN Berkeley Square,* some years since, lived Mr. Johnson, a gentleman of noble descent, of most respectable connexions, and possessing in Yorkshire a landed property,* which yielded to him a clear annual income of ten thousand pounds, besides a seat in parliament for a borough belonging to the estate.* He had a son, named Henry, who, being his only child, engrossed all the care of his fondly affectionate father and mother. No expense was spared on his education: masters of first-rate abilities were employed to instruct him in every branch of knowledge requisite to make him a complete gentleman, and qualify him to shine at court and in parliament: and, besides the pains bestowed on him by his different teachers, his parents also devoted to his instruction and improvement every moment which they could spare from the avocations* unavoidably incident to persons of their rank and fortune.

Master Harry was a lad of good natural talents: he possessed a clear understanding, as he often proved by the shrewd, sensible remarks which he occasionally made on the objects and transactions around him: he also had a retentive memory; for he could long and correctly remember any conversation or occurrence which had particularly attracted his attention, or pleased his fancy.

With such advantages from nature, fortune, and parental care, it was reasonable to expect that Master Harry should have made a most rapid progress in his learning; and so he certainly would have done, but for one unfortunate circumstance. Like some other young gentlemen of that and the present time, Master Harry had an unconquerable aversion to his books. The silly boy foolishly imagined, that, because he was born heir to an ample estate, and was sure of a permanent seat in parliament, he had no occasion for learning, which he thought only fit for poor men, who earned their bread by teaching, or by writing books for the amusement of idle gentlemen.

His parents and his teachers used every argument in their power, to convince him, that, without learning, he never could expect to shine as a gentleman; and that an illiterate man of fortune is not more respected than his footman or his groom. But they talked to no purpose: for Master Harry was obstinately determined not to learn; and, though he betrayed no symptoms of sulkiness or ill-humour at their admonitions, yet their words were no sooner spoken, than forgotten. So far was he from taking any pains to study his lessons in his book, that he would not even lend his ear to admit that knowledge which he might have acquired without the trouble of study, by only listening to the remarks that his teachers made to him. While they were vainly laboring to instruct him, his thoughts were wholly bent on toys and play; and, whenever a question was put to him respecting his lesson, he answered, at random, any nonsense that first came into his head, without caring what it was; and plainly proved, by the preposterous absurdity of his replies, that he did not think it worth his while to attend to a single word of what was said to him. So persevering was he in his obstinate determination not to learn, that, at the end of twelve months from his entrance on the grammar, he either could not or would not even enumerate the parts of speech, or tell the difference between a noun and a verb: and, during the subsequent years, his progress was no better than might naturally have been expected from so unpromising a commencement.

A sad young rogue he was, thus sinfully to waste his precious time, together with large sums of his father's money, which might have been so much better employed in relieving the wants of his distressed fellow creatures: and such criminal conduct deserved, no doubt, to be severely punished. Let not *us*, however, be too hasty to inflict punishment: for "vengeance is mine,'" says the Lord, "who willeth not the death of the sinner, but rather that he be converted, and live.'" To God, therefore, let us leave him—only observing, that, while he was thus shamefully and wickedly squandering his valuable days, and with cruel ingratitude wounding the hearts of his affectionate parents, who were grieved almost to distraction by his obstinate neglect of his studies, Mr. Wilmore, a distant relative of the family, by the assistance of an ingenious attorney, discovered a flaw in Mr. Johnson's title to the Yorkshire estate, and immediately commenced a suit, to wrest it from him.

After a tedious and expensive process in Chancery,* which continued during several successive years, the property was finally adjudged to Mr. Wilmore; and Mr. Johnson lost, not only the possession, but, together with it, his seat also in the house of commons: for, the parliament being dissolved about that time, and a new election ensuing, Mr. Wilmore, now proprietor of the estate, was of course returned member for the borough belonging to it.

The expenses of the Chancery suit had devoured considerable sums of money; so that Mr. Johnson, though ever accustomed to live within the bounds of his income, had but a very scanty supply of cash remaining in the hands of his banker at the time when he lost possession of the Yorkshire estate. Thus circumstanced, he felt himself extremely embarrassed, and was for some time unable to determine what course he should thenceforward pursue. But, while anxiously deliberating on the choice of a plan, and considering how he might best provide for the future subsistence and welfare of his son, an event occurred, which materially influenced and hastened his determination.

Some years before, he had become surety,* to a considerable amount, for Mr. Freeport, a merchant in the City, who was connected by marriage with a distant branch of his family: and, to complete the measure of his calamities, Mr. Freeport having lately been ruined by an unsuccessful speculation in trade, that gentleman's creditors now came upon Mr. Johnson, to recover the sum for which he had passed his security. The money in the hands of his banker, far from being adequate to meet this sudden and un-expected demand, was scarcely sufficient to pay his own debts to his different tradesmen. Such a host of misfortunes, all together crowding upon him as if by concert, would have tempted a man of less integrity to disappoint his creditors, and avoid paying his debts: but Mr. Johnson, being a gentleman of strict honor, determined to satisfy every claimant, even if absolute beggary were to be the consequence. For the accomplishment of that noble resolve, he was obliged to sell, not only his sheep and oxen in Yorkshire, but also his horses and his carriages, his plate and his costly furniture, together with his elegant house in Berkeley Square. Even his wife's jewels were not spared: and, when all was sold, and every debt paid, he had exactly three hundred pounds remaining.

Three hundred pounds are but a scanty pittance:* yet, to some men of abilities, they would prove a fortune, and would enable them, in a few years, to acquire considerable wealth, and ride independent in their carriages. Luckily, indeed, Mr. Johnson was not deficient in endowments, natural or acquired: besides being a very excellent scholar, he had a remarkable taste for painting, with a happy talent for taking likenesses, and had, for his amusement, at different times, drawn pictures of all his intimate acquaintance, which were much admired, not only by his friends, but even by professed artists, whom the spirit of rivalry would naturally render less disposed to flatter him.*

Had he offered his services to the public as a portrait-painter, there could have been no doubt of his acquiring money sufficient to live, if not in his former affluence and splendor, at least in very comfortable mediocrity. But he felt his pride so severely hurt at the idea of being employed for hire by those persons with whom he had formerly associated upon terms of equality, and even by his inferiors, that he could not brook* the thought of making the attempt in England. Hearing, however, that portrait-painters were very scarce and very well paid in America, he resolved to seek refuge and employment in that distant quarter of the globe.

Accordingly, he first provided himself with a sufficient stock of colors, pencils, and every other article requisite for the profession which he intended to embrace: he next set apart a sum to purchase sea-stores, pay his passage across the Atlantic, and leave in his pocket a few guineas for immediate use on his landing in America; and, with the residue, he purchased an assortment of cutlery, from which he had been taught to expect a handsome profit* on his arrival in Philadelphia; for which place he set sail,* with his wife and son, about the end of May.

They commenced their voyage with a fair wind, and, for ten days, steadily pursued their due course. During that time, no event occurred worthy of notice, except the appearance of a beautiful phænomenon, which is sometimes observed at sea, though very rarely; for it very rarely happens that the causes, which together combine to give it existence, are found to co-operate precisely within the sphere of the navigator's observation. On this occasion, they did co-operate:—the wind blowing pretty fresh, and the sun shining extremely bright—the wind, moreover, happening to form with the sun the exact angle requisite to produce the wondrous effect—innumerable small rainbows were seen at once starting up to view, and vanishing, in rapid succession—all within a limited space in the quarter opposed to the sun— where the showery spray of each wave, as tossed from its curling top by the wind, offered to the astonished sight the momentary exhibition of a perfect rainbow, though of diminished size.* The enjoyment of this magnificent spectacle continued for a considerable time, until, the sun having risen beyond a certain altitude, and ceased to form the proper angle on the spray, the watery mirror no longer reflected his rays in the same manner to the navigator's eye.

A few days after this, a calm of some hours' continuance afforded an opportunity of trying a curious experiment.—An empty quart bottle being closely corked, the cork and mouth were well coated with pitch, and cov- ered with a piece of strong sail-cloth, tightly strained, and fast tied round the neck. This covering being also pitched, the bottle was let down into the water, and, by means of a heavy leaden weight, sunk to the depth of about sixty fathoms.

During the preparations that were made for this experiment, some of the passengers asserted that the bottle would be crushed to pieces by the irre- sistible pressure of the water at so great a depth: others maintained that the roundness of its shape would enable it to resist the pressure. Mr. Johnson gave an opinion quite different from either, but was laughed at by both parties. At length, however, the bottle was drawn up; and, agreeably to Mr. Johnson's prediction, it came up safe, sound, and full of water. The water which it contained, was much cooler than that of the surface of the ocean; the influence of the solar rays being unable to penetrate to so great a depth.—The cork had been driven into the bottle, though, to all appearance, no human power could have forced it down in the open air, without bursting the neck. The canvas too, though so tightly strained and so securely bound, had been forced about half an inch down into the neck of the bottle: but the coating of pitch remained un-injured, and betrayed not the smallest visible aperture, that could have been supposed to have admitted the water, which therefore must have forced its way through the invisible pores of the pitch, as mercury, by the aid of the air-pump, is made to force its way through the pores of wood.*

Soon after this experiment, a favorable breeze sprang up, which continued without variation for several days; and, after three weeks of prosperous navigation, Mr Johnson had the pleasure of learning from the captain that the ship had now performed half her course, and that, if the wind continued equally propitious, he hoped, in three weeks more, to drop anchor in Delaware bay.* Enlivened by this agreeable intelligence, and having, at that season of the year, every reasonable prospect of happily terminating his voyage, he indulged himself at dinner with an extra glass from his scanty store of wine, allowed himself a similar indulgence at supper, and, at a late hour, retired to rest, as happy and contented as a man in his circumstances could be supposed to be.

Pleasing dreams ensued.—He fancied himself already settled in Philadelphia, and that he had just finished a portrait of General Washington, which gave such universal satisfaction, that the Congress immediately passed a resolution for employing him to draw likenesses of all the surviving members of the old Congress who had first voted the independence of America.* These pictures, he thought, were intended to adorn the federal hall;* and a considerable sum was voted for that purpose. Cheered by the prospect which now opened before him, he felt himself as happy at this moment as at any former period in his whole life. Already, from the fancied profits of his new profession, he had ideally purchased, at a cheap rate, a princely extent of territory in the back country of Kentucky,* which, in a few years, would by far outvalue his late possessions in Yorkshire: already, in fond imagination, he saw his posterity members of Congress,* and one of them even a candidate for the presidency of the United States, with a strong probability of success in his pursuit.

But, in the midst of these pleasing delusions, he was suddenly roused from his slumbers before day-break, by a tumultuous uproar, and the hasty trampling of feet over his head; when, starting instantly from his couch, and running up on deck, he heard several voices crying out that the vessel was sinking; and, by the light of the moon, which then shone very bright, he saw the crew preparing to hoist out the boats, and abandon the ship.

Harry, too, having been disturbed by the noise, rose from his bed, and followed his father to the deck; where, hearing of the danger to which the vessel was exposed, he was sorely terrified. He shuddered at the idea of being devoured alive by sharks and other monsters of the deep: but he was still more afraid of what might befall him in the other world after death. His perverse and wanton waste of his time now rushed back in terrors upon his recollection; and he dreaded the severest punishment from the wrath of God, who will demand a strict account of all our moments, and will reward or punish us according as we have well or ill spent that time which he has allotted to us upon earth. He now would gladly have recalled those lost hours and days and years, that he might better employ them: but those hours and days and years were all irrevocably fled, and had left him nought behind but stupid ignorance and un-availing regret.

As to his father, *he* was not alarmed at the thoughts of death. He had ever been a good and virtuous man: he had not to reproach himself with any crime: and the good man, whose conscience is free from guilt, is not afraid of that grim phantom, Death, whom he considers only as the friendly usher who is to introduce him to the presence of his almighty father and sovereign in a better world, where he is sure of being rewarded for his meritorious deeds.

If the transit from this to the other life be sometimes painful, he knows that the pain unlocks the door to future joy; and he resignedly submits to it, as the way-worn traveler, returning to his wished-for home, submits to the jolting and spattering of a rugged, dirty road, and to all the inclemencies of the weather—because he well knows, that, without reconciling himself to these temporary inconveniences, he cannot expect to enjoy those lasting pleasures which await him on his arrival. Perhaps even, after the calamities that he had suffered, and the melancholy reverse which had taken place in his fortune, death might have been more welcome to Mr. Johnson, than life; though, with the resignation of a true Christian, he thought it his duty to acquiesce in the dispensations of heaven, and patiently to bear the burden of an irksome existence, as long as it should please the Almighty to protract its duration; without daring to rebel against his maker, and meanly to escape from the pressure of adversity by a cowardly act of suicide:* for cowardly he deemed it, as well as impious, and was often heard to repeat two excellent lines of the pagan poet, Martial, importing, that, when Fortune frowns, no great courage is shown in daring to die, but true courage consists in daring to live †.*

But, though not afraid of simple death, Mr. Johnson was shocked at the idea of being obliged to quit the sinking vessel, and commit himself, with a beloved wife and child, to a small boat, to row fifteen hundred miles on the dreary ocean, whether they directed their course for Europe or America— or, at least, five or six hundred, if they steered for the Azores, or Western Islands,* which were then the nearest land. The hardships of such a voyage in an open boat, without a covering to shelter them from the wind or rain, or from the dashing of the Atlantic waves, must have been dreadful beyond conception to a lady and a child so delicately reared as they had been, and accustomed to every indulgence that wealth could procure. Still more dreadful, however, was the idea, that, after having been tossed by contrary winds for several weeks, they might at last be reduced to the alternative of either perishing by hunger, or casting lots to determine which of the unfortunate sufferers should be killed, that the survivors might feed upon his flesh—a dire alternative, to which wretched mariners have sometimes been driven!*

Such were the torturing reflexions which now crowded upon Mr. Johnson's mind. Afraid, however, of increasing the terror of his wife and child, he mastered his feelings on this trying occasion, and did not, by a single word or look, betray the painful sensations which harrowed up his soul; but silently looked around him, observing every thing that was said or done, that he might the more clearly discover the true state of the case.

On the deck stood the captain, whose countenance displayed that cool determined courage which is the natural result of habitual acquaintance with danger. Full oft, amid the uproar of Atlantic storms, he had, with the eye of fancy, beheld gigantic Death striding over the tops of the mountain billows, and each moment threatening to invade his defenceless ship: but he had learned to behold him without a single sensation of unmanly terror; and, on the present occasion, he was seen calmly giving his orders to the tumultuous crew, and chiding them for their over-hasty alarm. He consented to the boats being cleared, and put into a state of readiness, but forbade them to be hoisted out. Tackles were accordingly prepared; and the boats were securely slung, to be ready for the last emergency; after which, he ordered the carpenter, with all the hands who could be spared from the deck, to go down into the hold, and endeavour to detect the cause of the mischief.

---

† Rebus in angustis facile est contemnere vitam.
   Fortiter ille facit, qui miser esse potest.

On examination, the danger did not appear so imminent as had, in the first moments of terror, been apprehended: yet it proved sufficiently serious to alarm the boldest mariner on board. During the night, the end of a plank in the fore part of the vessel had started from its fastenings; and the water was seen rushing with great violence through the opening, though not in such quantity as to threaten immediate submersion. Upon this discovery, the captain instantly ordered a spare sail to be produced; and, having directed a sufficient portion of it to be thickly covered with locks of oakum,* hastily sewed on, and well smeared with grease and tar, he caused it to be drawn down over the chink, and secured with ropes passing under the ship's bottom. This being done, the weight of the sea pressing against the sail as the vessel moved forward, so far closed the aperture with the oakum, that there was no longer any danger of the water coming in faster than the crew could pump it out, provided they used due diligence.

That innate love of life, which the Almighty has, for a wise purpose, implanted in the heart of every animated being, spurred them on to make their utmost exertions: four men were incessantly employed at the pumps by day and by night, to keep the ship afloat; and, such critical emergencies admitting no distinction or respect of persons, Mr. Johnson and the other male passengers were obliged to take their turn with the common sailors at the laborious drudgery of working the pumps.

At length, after severe distress, fatigue, and alarm, the vessel safely anchored in the Delaware, and Mr. Johnson, with his family, landed at Philadelphia about the twentieth of July. Here he learned with pleasure that his boxes of cutlery promised to prove a lucrative speculation; and he soon found a person willing to purchase them at even a higher price than he had been taught to expect. What, therefore, must have been his feelings, when, eagerly hasting to unpack the boxes, he found their contents all damaged by the salt water which had made its way into the ship's hold, and so much depreciated by that unfortunate event, that, instead of gaining by the sale, he lost above two thirds of the money which the goods had originally cost him!

In *his* circumstances, this was a severe stroke; and it sorely preyed upon his spirits, which were already broken down, as well by his misfortune in England, as by the fatigue of pumping, and the want of rest, during the latter half of the voyage. Nor was this the whole of his calamity: it was now the middle of the dog-days*—the most dangerous time of the year for an unseasoned European to arrive in America. Had he deferred his voyage for a couple of months, and contrived to land there after the middle or end of September, all might yet have been well. But his eager impatience to escape from the insulting sneers of some of his former acquaintance, and the no less insulting pity of others, had urged him to accelerate his departure, without sufficiently considering the effects of climate or season: and now, bodily fatigue and vexation of spirit being joined to the intolerable dog-day heat of a sultry clime, he was seised* by a violent fever, which carried him off within a fortnight after his arrival.

Happy for him was the transit from a world of woe to a world of bliss; but not so for his widowed wife and orphan child, whom he thus left helpless and friendless in a strange land. Mrs. Johnson did not long survive him, but died of a broken heart in less than three months from the day of his decease. After the loss on the sale of the cutlery, and the un-avoidable expenses of sickness, there remained little more money in young Harry's possession at the time of her death, than was sufficient to defray the charges of her funeral, even in that country, where neither mutes nor hearses nor mourning-coaches* are seen in the funeral procession, but a sober, solemn, un-expensive simplicity characterises the last awful ceremony of consigning a departed friend to the grave.

Harry was now about fourteen years old, an almost pennyless stranger in a foreign land, deprived of the last friend to whom he could have looked up for aid and protection. His grief for the loss of so affectionate a mother would, under any circumstances, have been great; but, in his present condition, it was great beyond conception. Having accompanied her remains to the place of burial—on seeing the coffin let down into the grave, he uttered a loud shriek of wild despair, which pierced the heart of every person present, and particularly attracted the attention of the clergyman who was reading the funeral service.

Less boisterous, though not less sincere, was the grief of Dick Hobson at the burial of *his* mother. Dick was the son of Thomas Hobson, Mr. Johnson's cowherd on the Yorkshire estate—and was of nearly the same age as Master Harry, having been born about a month after him. Two years before Mr. Johnson's departure from England, Dick had witnessed the death of his mother, who, though a low-bred, ignorant peasant, had nevertheless been to him a tender and affectionate parent. Dick loved her sincerely, sincerely regretted her loss, and, when he attended her remains to the grave, wept bitterly indeed, but wept in silence, without uttering either a shriek or a word. Young as he was, he had learned to consider death in its true light, as only a passage to a better world: and, although he could not forbear to indulge his natural affection for his mother by shedding a flood of tears; yet the consolatory reflexion, that she was gone to receive the reward of her humble virtues in a place where she should never more experience poverty or pain, restrained him from breaking out into any noisy exclamations of intemperate grief.

From *Learning better than House and Land* (2nd ed.; London, 1810)

Such philosophic resignation, blended with such tender sensibility, would have done honor to the head and the heart of the best educated youth of his years: it was still more admirable in the son of a cow-herd. But, however mean his birth and condition, he had, by a fortunate and singular concurrence of events, been blest with advantages in point of education, which rarely fall to the lot of persons in his lowly sphere. His father, it is true, was an illiterate rustic, who knew as little of reading or writing as any one of the cows intrusted to his care: but he was a sober, sensible, prudent man, affectionately attached to his son, and anxiously ambitious to promote the boy's welfare and advancement in the world:—in short, Thomas Hobson was, in every acceptation of the word, a very good father, who might have served as a model to many fathers of much superior rank. Ignorant as he was himself, he had heard so much of the advantages of learning, that he had early determined to give Dick as large a portion of it as he could afford. Accordingly, as soon as the child had reached the age of five years, he sent him to the village school,* kept by Mr. Wilson, to whom he paid three pence per week for his education.

Inheriting his father's disposition, and taught by his example, Dick was careful, attentive, and diligent. Being fond of his book, he soon learned to spell and read, and made uncommonly rapid progress in his learning, insomuch that, before he was seven years old, he could read the common prayer and lessons at church as fluently as the parish clerk, and correctly pronounce many hard names in the Bible, which might perhaps have puzzled even a better scholar than the parish clerk. In process of time, young Dick was taught writing and arithmetic: and so fond was he of handling his pen, that, whenever he received a few halfpence from any gentleman whose horse he had happened to hold, or for whom he had opened a gate, he instantly ran to lay out the money in paper, and amused himself with writing during his leisure hours at home. Before he was ten years old, he had, besides a variety of other pieces, copied out, in a fair hand, the entire history of Joseph and his brethren from the Bible, and that of Whittington and his cat from a little penny book which his father had purchased for him at a fair. He was particularly delighted with Whittington's history,* which showed that even a beggar may sometimes, by attentive industry, raise himself from poverty to wealth and greatness.

In arithmetic he made a remarkable proficiency, and, by the age of eleven, was perfectly acquainted with all the common rules, insomuch that Mr. Wilson, his master, was glad of his assistance in teaching the younger boys; in return for which service, he now not only taught Dick for nothing, but paid extraordinary attention to his improvement.

[48]

THE EDUCATION OF DICK HOBSON

From *Learning better than House and Land* (2nd ed.; London, 1810)

Fortunate was Dick in being placed under the care of such a man: for Mr. Wilson, though a poor village school-master, possessed more knowledge than some teachers in great towns and cities; and he took particular pleasure in communicating that knowledge to so apt a pupil as Dick, who, in due time, learned from him all the rules of vulgar and decimal fractions, and became a tolerable proficient in book-keeping.

Mr. Wilson, moreover, seeing how fond the boy was of reading, had lent to him, one after the other, every book in his little library, which consisted of about forty volumes; and these Dick had read through with great avidity and attention, carefully enriching his mind with their valuable contents.

Forty volumes, however, were far from sufficient to satisfy Dick's thirst of knowledge: and, as he approached the end of his career through Mr. Wilson's library, he was often heard to express his regret that his progress should so soon be stopped for want of a further supply of books.

Luckily, however, for Dick, an event occurred about this period, which, for a time, relieved his mind from all anxiety on the subject of reading. William Brown, his maternal uncle, came to settle in his father's neighbour-hood. Several years before, Brown had enlisted in the army as a common soldier; and, being soon noticed by his officers as a sober, steady, orderly man, he had hopes given him of being raised to the rank of corporal, if he could but read and write.* Poor Brown could do neither: but, unwilling that his ignorance should prove a bar to his preferment, he purchased instruction from one of his comrades, at the expense of occasionally doing duty for him, and cleaning his arms and accoutrements. He thus attained the object of his wishes, was in due time appointed corporal, and, having distinguished him-self by his good conduct in the American war,* was further promoted to the rank of serjeant. He had received some wounds in the service, and, being now discharged on a pension, returned to spend the remainder of his days in his native village, carrying with him in the waggon a small trunk of books, which had been bequeathed to him, together with some clothes and money, by an officer of his regiment, who died on board the ship on the passage home from America, and whose life he had formerly saved in battle, at the risk of his own.

This trunk of books proved a treasure to Dick: his uncle allowed him the free use of them all; and Dick eagerly availed himself of that indulgence. Nor did his good fortune end here. His passion for learning was further gratified by Mr. Penrose, a reduced gentleman,* who came to board at a neighbour-ing farm-house, and for whom he occasionally went on errands to the market-town, a few miles distant. That gentleman had a small, but well chosen, collection of books—a circumstance, which eventually proved advantageous to Dick: for Mr. Penrose—being highly pleased with the lad's cheerfulness and punctuality in executing his various commissions, and having understood that he was fond of reading—determined to indulge him in that respect, if he found that he could do it with safety. Accordingly, as a trial, he first ventured to trust him with a volume of trifling value; after which, on finding that the youth returned it within a reasonable time perfectly safe and clean, he lent him others in succession. Dick profited so well by this advantage, that, at the time of his mother's death, when he was only twelve years old, he was tolerably well acquainted with history and geography, had pretty accurate notions of English grammar, and reasoned on religious subjects with a correctness which could hardly have been expected at his age. Hence that exemplary behaviour at his mother's funeral, which at once proved him to be an affectionate son, and a pious, rational Christian.

Such was Dick, but considerably improved, and still daily improving, when, at the age of fourteen, he saw his father suddenly dismissed from his employment, in consequence of 'Squire Johnson's losing the estate, and selling off the cattle to pay his debts.

Old Hobson, though sincerely grieved for the misfortune which had befallen a good and kind master, did not feel any great regret on his own or his son's account. They were not left destitute: for Thomas, being a sober, economic man, had, partly from his own earnings and perquisites* during a long series of years spent in 'Squire Johnson's service, partly from his wife's earnings and a couple of small legacies, contrived to save upwards of a hundred pounds, which he kept carefully concealed under the hearth-stone in his cottage, in solid, heavy guineas. With that sum, he might have taken a small farm in the neighbourhood: but his brother-in-law, Serjeant Brown, had given him so pleasing an account of America—had so extolled the cheapness and fertility of the soil, and the ease with which any man can there gain a comfortable livelihood, who is at all able and willing to work—that he had long been determined to remove with his son to that happy region, and only waited to add a few pounds more to the hundred which he had already amassed.

His sudden dismissal, however, wrought a change in his intentions: he at once renounced the idea of staying any longer in England to increase his wealth, and resolved not to try a new master, but to embark for America by the first opportunity. Accordingly, having disposed of his cottage with what little furniture it contained, and carefully sewed up his guineas in the back of his waistcoat, he set out on foot with his son Dick, and, after three days' march, safely reached the town of Hull, where he found a vessel preparing to sail for New York.

Having first agreed with the captain for his own and his son's passage in the steerage,* and paid the price in advance, he next proceeded, agreeably to Serjeant Brown's directions, to lay out the remainder of his money (with the reserve of only three guineas) in the purchase of such articles as he should himself have occasion for in America, or might sell to advantage on his arrival. Those three guineas, which he reserved, and still kept safe in the back of his waistcoat, were intended as a provision against unforeseen expenses on his landing, not for the purchase of sea-stores: for Thomas and his son— being, both, hale and hearty, and having been accustomed to hard living— did not require delicacies, but were content to live with the sailors on the common ship's fare.

The vessel having taken in her cargo, and every thing being now ready, Thomas and his son embarked, and proceeded on their voyage, about a month previous to Mr. Johnson's departure from England.

They had not been many days at sea, when a remarkable mortality took place among the fowls which the cabin passengers had brought on board, as provision for the voyage. But a circumstance, even more remarkable than the mortality itself, was, that the fowls always died in the night; hardly a night passing, which did not witness the death of one or two of their number.

When first these sudden deaths were announced, the passengers, influenced by that disgust which Englishmen habitually harbour against the flesh of any creature that has died of old age or disease, ordered the dead fowls to be thrown overboard: but the mate opportunely interposed to save them, observing to the gentlemen that common sailors were not over-nice in that respect—that even the dead fowls would be a treat to the crew, and the poor fellows would be glad to eat them with their salt beef. Permission was accordingly granted; and, as a fowl or two died almost every night, the "poor fellows" had, almost every day, a fowl or two for dinner; while the gentlemen in the cabin did not always allow themselves that indulgence, for fear of too rapidly consuming their stock, which was already beginning to be very sensibly diminished by those nightly deaths, added to the daily consumption at the cabin table.

In this train matters proceeded for a fortnight: various were the causes assigned for that un-accountable mortality; various were the remedies proposed; but no expedient could be devised, to check its progress. At the end of that time, however, Thomas Hobson discovered both the cause and the cure.

Having accidentally overheard the conversation of two of the sailors, he clearly learned from it that they themselves designedly killed the fowls during the night, with the certain expectation of feasting on them at dinner the next day, as they well knew from experience that genteel cabin passengers would never consent to taste a fowl which they supposed to be tainted with disease: and the mate, it seems, was not only privy to the roguish scheme, but active, moreover, in promoting its success.

Although Thomas was a gainer by this knavish trick of the sailors, who allowed him a share of the fowls at dinner, yet his strong sense of honesty prompted him to impart this discovery to the cabin passengers, who thereupon held a private consultation, and formed a counter-scheme, to save the remainder of their fowls from those nocturnal depredators.

Pursuant to their pre-concerted plan—when next they were informed that two had died during the night, "Gentlemen," said Mr. Green to his fellow passengers in the hearing of the crew, "it is well known that the Chinese unscrupulously feed on the flesh of animals that have died a natural death;* nor do we learn that any harm or inconvenience ensues from the use of such food. What does not poison a Chinese, can hardly poison an Englishman: at all events, let us try: and, if we dislike the fowls when cooked, let us throw them overboard; for I cannot approve the idea of suffering the honest tars to feed on what we should deem unwholesome for ourselves....What say you, gentlemen?"

The proposal being unanimously applauded—the dead fowls being eaten in the cabin—and the sailors seeing that they no longer had any hope of deriving advantage from their roguery—the nightly mortality all at once ceased; and, from that time forward, not another fowl died on the passage, except under the cook's knife.

Some unthinking people, who have not proper notions of right and wrong, would consider Thomas Hobson as a fool, for making a disclosure, by which he was himself likely to be a loser. But Thomas, though an illiterate peasant, had more correct ideas on the subject, than they: for he had, even from his childhood, been punctually regular in joining the congregation at church on Sundays, and had carefully attended to the sound practical doctrine preached by a truly pious and sensible pastor. Taught by that worthy man, and further confirmed in his opinion by those moral and religious books which his son had been used to read to him at leisure hours, he rightly considered, that, whether we lose or gain by honest upright conduct, it is our incumbent duty to pursue it at all events: and he was frequently heard to say, that, though knavery may *sometimes* thrive for *a while*, yet, in the main, honesty is the safest policy, and will always succeed best in the end.

So indeed it happened on this occasion: for the cabin passengers, in grateful acknowledgement of Hobson's disinterested integrity, every day took care to send to him from their own table a plate of something much better than the common ship's fare. At the same time, to punish the mate for his

criminal connivance at the sailors' roguery, and the deception he had practised on themselves by his insidious suggestions respecting the disposal of the
dead fowls, they never once, during the remainder of the voyage, treated
him with a single glass of their wines or *liqueurs*, or imparted to him the
smallest share of their fowls or other delicacies.*

While he and his nightly ravagers of the hen-coop were silently grieving
for the loss of their wonted regales* at the passengers' expense, a ravager of a
different species made his appearance.—"A shark! a shark!" cried one of the
men upon watch—"A shark! a shark!" echoed from every part of the ship; and
in an instant the passengers were all upon deck, to view the formidable foe.

At a small distance astern, he steadily followed the vessel, and seemed
fiercely to eye his beholders, as if indignant that he could not spring out of
the water, to seise his prey on the very deck. But he little knew that he was
himself in greater danger than they—little knew the immense superiority
which God has given to the human species over every other class of animated nature—a superiority resulting from that inestimable gift, the intellectual faculty, which enables feeble diminutive man to subdue the largest,
the strongest, the fiercest of the brute creation.

Preparations were speedily made to catch the monster. Connected with
a strong line by four or five feet of iron chain, a large hook, baited with a
couple of pounds of salt pork, was thrown out into the waves. It had not
long floated in the water, till the shark, slowly turning up his breast, and
bending back his head, wide opened his capacious jaws, and quickly closed
them on the bait. The men who had charge of the line, being inexperienced
in shark-catching, pulled the rope before he had completely gulped down
the pork: the hook tore his jaw: his blood was seen to tinge the waters: but
the felon himself was not taken.

Had this ravager possessed the sagacity of a dog or a cat, or even of an ass,
all might yet have been well with him, and he might have escaped at the
expense of that laceration and loss of blood. But wisely and mercifully has
the Almighty ordained that the most destructive animals should be deficient
in some quality which would render them too surely, too extensively
destructive—should be swayed by some propensity, or checked by some
incapacity, which either throws them into the power of man, or at least
enables man and other creatures to elude their rapacious fury.

The effect of that wise dispensation was clearly shown by the shark in
question.—On receiving the wound, he shook his head, wagged his tail,
turned away from the ship, and, for a while, seemed disposed to renounce
the hope of prey. But this disposition did not long continue: for, before he
had retreated from the navigators' sight, he again turned to the vessel, again

followed it, first at some distance, then, more nearly approaching, again rushed on the bait. Again he was wounded: again he escaped as before; and, after a repetition of the same procedure on his part, the same thing happened a third time. Three times was he hooked and lacerated: three times was his blood distinctly seen to flow: yet so greedy was his rapacity, so gross his stupidity, that, even after those repeated admonitions, he could not consent to relinquish the tempting lure.

On the third failure, a passenger, who had never before seen a shark, and who was almost frantic with disappointed impatience, ran to the captain, who had retired to write in the cabin during that quiet interval of leisure and silence which the general absence of the passengers afforded him. He now interrupted his writing, and quickly repaired to the quarter-deck,* to superintend the operations.

A fourth time the monster snatched at the bait; when, instead of hastily pulling the rope as before, the sailors were now directed to give out plenty of line. On swallowing the meat, the shark instantly turned tail upon the vessel, and was deliberately sailing off—little aware of what was shortly to ensue. When he had reached the full extent of the line, the sudden shock of resistance fastened the hook deep into his maw, and, with a rapid jerk, forcibly whirled him round. The felon was now inextricably secured: but it would have been too dangerous to have immediately taken him on board the vessel. He was suffered to hang on the hook; and, in spite of his angry efforts to bite asunder the iron chain, he was reluctantly dragged along, plunging and writhing in agony, until his strength was in some degree exhausted by his unavailing struggles.

When at length it was deemed safe to drag the captive on board, the line was pulled in, and he was hauled to the ship's side: then, a running noose being dextrously placed round his throat, and another round his body—and the other end of each rope being passed through a block (or pulley) at the yard-arm*—his own weight drawing the nooses tight, he was hoisted out of his native element, while a sufficient number of men, properly armed for his reception, stood posted on the main deck, but at cautious distance. When lowered upon deck, they all together rushed on him with boat-hooks and spears, and, overpowering his furious resistance, pinned him down to the board, though not without exposing themselves to danger in their first onset.

When a shark is thus secured, it is customary to rip him open, and examine the contents of his maw. In the present case, that bloody operation was duly performed; and, during its performance, the agonised monster made violent and convulsive struggles to liberate himself from confinement, and wreak his vengeance on his torturers. With the lashing of his tail on the

THE SHARK TAKEN

From *Learning better than House and Land* (2nd ed.; London, 1810)

deck, he made the ship resound; and, while his eyes seemed starting out of his head with rage, he made repeated efforts to heave himself up, and tear the persons nearest to him—wide stretching his terrific jaws, and displaying five rows of strong sharp teeth*—each shaped like a surgeon's lancet, and minutely notched along the edges like a fine saw—which were seen starting up for action as he opened his mouth, and again falling flat upon the gums as he closed it.

Armed with such destructive teeth, and endued with prodigious muscular power in the jaws, no wonder that the shark can bite off a man's leg or thigh with as great ease (if the reader will excuse the comparison) as a cow can bite a carrot. But, confined as he now was, neither his teeth nor his muscular powers aught availed him. His maw was opened and ransacked; and the first objects, which there presented themselves to view, exhibited a convincing proof that the shark does not chew his food, but gulps it down in great solid mouthfuls, like those voracious clowns* in some parts of England, who *bolt* down their bacon in large gobbets,* without employing their teeth.

Those objects—exclusive of the bait, for which he paid his forfeit life— were two other pieces of pork, each about the same size as that which our navigators had successfully used in decoying him to his doom. Of these, the one was perfectly sound and un-injured: the other, though slightly affected on the surface by the digestive powers of the stomach, still retained its original form and solidity; and both together furnished unquestionable evidence that they had not undergone the process of mastication.

Besides these, another object was discovered—a gold watch, with its chain and seals.—Though it appeared, on examination, that the works of the watch had been materially impaired by lying a considerable time in the shark's maw, yet the number and maker's name* were still perfectly legible: and, exclusive of these evidences, the owner's name on the gold case, with his cipher and crest* on the seals, would have been more than sufficient to lead to a discovery. Accordingly, it was soon recognised by a gentleman on board, as the identical watch that he himself, about two years before, had given to his only son, a promising youth of eighteen, then setting out on a West-India voyage, in which he unfortunately fell overboard, and was drowned.*

The shock, which the hapless parent received on this heart-rending recognition, may more easily be conceived than described. Even the rough sailors sympathised with him; and their sympathy for him rendered them perhaps more alert and active in consummating the execution of the shark.

After the examination of his maw, they chopped off his head, which they kept, for the purpose of stripping and drying the jaws, to be preserved as a curiosity. And now, agreeably to the usual practice of navigators, the cook—

a West-Indian negro—was preparing to cut off a piece of a few pounds near the tail for the captain's table, and a much larger piece toward the middle for the ship's crew: but so great was the disgust and abhorrence of every white man on board to feed upon a monster which had evidently devoured one of their fellow men, that even the common sailors unanimously cried out to have the carcase thrown overboard. Otherwise, though coarse and rank, they would have made a hearty meal of it, and been as highly pleased to catch a shark every day, as are the Portuguese fishermen, who sell at least one species of shark for food in the market at Oporto.

Severe and painful as was the execution of the shark, that merciless destroyer may perhaps be thought to have justly deserved it. But, in the eye of the all-just Creator, who, with impartial care, equally watches over the welfare of all his creatures, such punishment would, no doubt, appear highly criminal, if inflicted on a poor harmless porpoise—which, far from being an enemy to man, may rather be considered as a friend to navigators, to whom, by his appearance, he gives notice of approaching storms,* and, on such occasions, by steering his course direct before the wind, marks the precise point of heaven whence the tempest is preparing to sally forth.

One day, while the ship was sailing right before a fresh breeze at the rate of full ten miles an hour, a party of those sportive creatures came to play their frolicsome gambols within sight. They crossed close under her bows—darted off to the right as far as the eye could trace them—then suddenly wheeling, again crossed her course—scudded as far to the left—and thus accompanied her during two or three hours, continually crossing and re-crossing, while the ship still pursued her rapid way at the same unvarying rate.

An observant passenger, who had stood near two hours on the forecastle* to watch their motions —considering, that, notwithstanding their long zig-zag deviations to the right and left, they still kept a-head of the vessel— declared his firm belief that they must have sailed at least thirty or forty miles an hour. Whether or not that gentleman was mistaken in his calculation— for it is utterly impossible to ascertain the point in question—most certain it is, that no terrestrial animal can at all equal the velocity of their course—nor any other fish, with which man is acquainted. With strict propriety, therefore, does the ingenious Mr. Falconer, in his elegant poem of the "Shipwreck,"* characterise the porpoises as

"the fleetest coursers of the finny race."

CANTO 2, 217.*

But their fleetness does not always secure them against the machinations of man, the universal tyrant of the brute creation. On the present occasion, some of the passengers having testified a wish to see one of them caught, the captain undertook to gratify them by striking one with a harpoon—the only mode, he said, of taking them, as he had never known a porpoise to catch at a bait of any kind.

The captain was a tall, muscular man, full six feet high—broad-built, robust, and powerful, in proportion to his size—and likewise a good marksman. For the execution of his purpose, he took his station at the bow, brandishing a barbed spear, or single-pronged harpoon, with a long shaft—not intended as a missile, but to be used as a hand-weapon. With this, exerting his utmost strength, he made a downward thrust at one of the poor harmless creatures, which had incautiously ventured too near the ship; and, with unerring aim, he inflicted on him a deep wound, as the sequel unquestionably proved.

The porpoise, however, escaped—having, by a sudden convulsive jerk, extricated himself from the barbed point of the spear. Yet he escaped not without loss in addition to the wound: for, when the weapon was drawn up, a piece of his entrails was seen sticking on the barbs. And such was the force with which he had darted aside on receiving the stroke, that it had considerably bent the round iron shank of the harpoon, though it was perhaps three quarters of an inch in diameter.

If the poor unfortunate porpoise had little reason to congratulate himself on his acquaintance with man, the captain had as little reason to boast of his exploit: for the shock, given by the wounded animal in that convulsive jerk, so jarred his arm and shoulder, that, for near a week, he could hardly lift his hand to his head without a sensation of pain—though not very violent or alarming, yet sufficient to revive an unpleasing recollection of the unprovoked and wanton aggression which he had made upon a poor un-offending porpoise.

No other remarkable event occurred to our voyagers during their passage across the Atlantic: pleasant and propitious gales securely wafted them over the broad bosom of the unfathomable deep, where neither rock nor shoal threatens the unwary mariner with shipwreck; and so favorable was the weather, that the captain disdained to adopt the cautious conduct of more timid commanders in uniformly slackening sail at the close of day, but boldly pursued his course by night under full-spread canvass; so that, after a prosperous run of thirty-one days, they had come into soundings* on the American coast.

Soon were their eyes feasted with a sight of the wished-for shore; and, at no great distance, the heights of New York rose to their view. Already, in fond anticipation, they enjoyed the exquisite pleasure of rest and refreshment on solid ground, and were now steering direct for the harbour, when a sudden squall un-expectedly made a furious attack upon their vessel, and, in spite of all the efforts of a skilful pilot seconded by a hardy and vigorous crew, drove her on shore upon the point of Long-Island,* where she was soon beaten to pieces by the violence of the waves.

The crew and passengers with difficulty effected their escape from the wreck, in the long-boat and yawl;* the former of which, after buffeting the boisterous billows for a considerable time, at length safely reached the island about sun-set; and, by the successful exertions of the islanders, the ship-wrecked sufferers were rescued from a watery grave. As to those in the yawl—just as they were on the point of gaining the beach, and a sailor had his hand outstretched to seise the end of a rope humanely thrown forward to them by a person on shore, a mountain surge, bursting over her, whelmed her in the deep; and every individual on board was swallowed up by the merciless waves.

Among the persons thus sunk in untimely death, was Thomas Hobson. His son Dick was among the survivors: for, in the hurry and confusion inseparable from such distressful scenes, Dick had instinctively jumped into the long-boat, and thus escaped a participation of his father's fate. To all appearance, however, it would have been a much more fortunate event for Dick, if he had accompanied his parent to the other world: for here the poor fellow now stood on a foreign shore, unknowing and unknown—suddenly deprived of a good and kind father, and no longer possessing any property under heaven, except the wet clothes on his back, and five shillings in his pocket, which he had received that morning from Mr. Nicols, one of the cabin passengers, as a remuneration for some little services which he had occasionally performed for that gentleman during the voyage.

Thus destitute as he was left in a strange land, the prospect before him was dismal in the extreme: but his grief for the untimely death of his father prevented him from yet bestowing a thought on his own misfortune. He suffered himself to be dragged from the spot by his companions in distress, whom the farmers of the vicinity, with that frank and generous hospitality for which the Americans are remarkable, had invited to take shelter in their houses. By these good men the unfortunate sufferers were furnished with dry clothes, comfortably lodged and entertained for the night; and, the next morning, after a hearty breakfast of coffee, eggs, sausages, dried fish, and smoked venison, they were conducted by their hosts to the landing-place, whence they crossed the ferry from Long-Island to New York.

Previous to his departure from the island, Dick had related his story to his hospitable entertainer, who directed him to a cheap lodging in the city, and advised him how to proceed. Agreeably to the farmer's directions, immediately on Dick's arrival in New York, his first care was to inquire for the printing-office, and put an advertisement into the newspaper,* offering his services as under clerk to any merchant or shop-keeper; and, even in the outset of the business, Dick was very fortunate: for the printer, understanding that he was a poor shipwrecked orphan, generously refused to accept the quarter-dollar which he must otherwise have paid for the advertisement. Pleased with this first instance of good fortune, Dick next sought the lodging-house to which he had been directed: and, as he had made so substantial a breakfast on Long-Island, he allowed himself no dinner, but fasted during the remainder of the day, with the view of economising his five shillings, and spinning out that scanty supply to the utmost length. At night he indulged himself with a light and un-expensive meal—the half of a penny loaf, and a draught of water; and, putting his trust in God, to whom he regularly addressed his prayers morning and evening, he retired to his humble couch, but not to sleep. His mind was too seriously occupied by the horrors of his present forlorn condition; and, however firm his confidence in the almighty goodness, however perfect his resignation to the divine will, he could not banish from his bosom the feelings of human nature. Bewildered in doubt and uncertainty—agitated by alternate hopes and fears—he anxiously awaited the return of day, to see whether his advertisement had produced any effect.

At eight o'clock the next morning, he repaired to the printing-office, but had the mortification to find that no inquiry had yet been made concerning him. The printer, however, afforded him a temporary consolation, by informing him that he was come too early—that the public had not yet had time to read the paper—but that, if he would call again after the lapse of two or three hours, perhaps he might then hear of something in his favor.

To poor Dick, that interval was an age. To fill up the time, he walked about the streets, and down by the water-side, admiring the noble and convenient wharfs, as well as the ease and regularity with which he saw numerous ships laden and unladen, without the smallest confusion or interference with each other. Attentive, however, as he was to these novel and interesting objects, he did not forget to watch the striking of the clock, but, precisely at ten, returned to the printing-office, without having yet broken his fast: for, although his walk by the water-side had whetted his appetite, which was naturally keen, and needed no provocative—and although, in his perambulation of the streets, he had passed the very door of his lodging—he had not ventured to touch the remaining half of his penny loaf, which he cautiously reserved to furnish his dinner—the only meal that he intended to allow himself that day.

From *Learning better than House and Land* (2nd ed.; London, 1810)

His second inquiry at the printing-office was productive of joy beyond expression: for he now learned that a note had been left about five minutes before, desiring the advertiser to call upon Mr. Harvey, an opulent merchant, whose place of abode was pointed out in the note.

Elate with this prospect of success, Dick ran, or rather flew, to the appointed place, but soon had the mortification to observe, that, on his very first appearance, the meanness of his dress, and the foulness of his linen, seemed (as he conjectured) to make an unfavorable impression upon Mr. Harvey's mind. Nor was Dick mistaken in his conjecture: for Mr. Harvey did indeed at first suppose that he certainly must be some graceless, worthless vagabond, or that he would otherwise be more decently dressed; and this idea had naturally caused him to view the poor fellow with unfriendly eye at the moment of his entrance. Being, however, a humane and considerate man, he determined not to be too hasty in condemning him at first sight, but to inquire who he was, and whence he came.

On learning the particulars of Dick's story, Mr. Harvey at once overlooked the circumstance of his dress, and, with great good-humour, proceeded to examine how far he was qualified to act in the capacity in which he wished to be employed. Dick instantly gave him a specimen of his writing, and had the exquisite gratification of hearing Mr. Harvey declare that it pleased him very well.—Some difficult questions in arithmetic were next proposed; and Dick, with the greatest ease and precision, solved them all to the merchant's entire satisfaction.

Mr. Harvey was, on the whole, very well pleased with the lad, and, pitying his distressed condition, would have been very willing to employ him: but to this there existed one material objection. To employ a stranger without character or recommendation, would have been highly imprudent. He mentioned this circumstance to Dick, and asked him whether he could name any person in America who knew any thing of him, or could speak a word in his favor.—Poor Dick, with a bursting heart, and the tears ready to start from his eyes, ingenuously acknowledged, that, except the captain and the surviving part of the passengers and crew who had been shipwrecked with him, there was not a human being in all America who knew any thing concerning him.

"Well!" replied Mr. Harvey, "I will hear what *they* say. This morning I shall see the captain at the exchange; and I know where to find some of the passengers. I shall have some conversation with them; and you may return again in the evening. Meantime, as you are, no doubt, in want of money for necessaries, I am willing to accommodate you with a small sum.

Here," added he, putting his hand into his pocket, and pulling out a doubloon*—"here, my good lad, take this, to purchase whatever you most stand in need of for the present."

Dick thanked him in terms of warmest gratitude for his generous offer, but declared that he was unwilling to contract debts, until he should see a probability of being able to repay them.—This answer highly pleased the merchant, and inspired him with a very favorable opinion of Dick's prudence and honesty, insomuch that, even before he saw the captain or passengers, he was almost determined to employ him. He, however, made inquiries of them in the course of the morning, and was so perfectly satisfied with the account which they unanimously gave of Dick's good behaviour on board the vessel, that he returned home to dinner with the fixed resolution of engaging the lad as his clerk that very day.

Before Dick's return, however, an occurrence took place, which produced a material change in Mr. Harvey,—quite ruffled his temper, and banished that cheerful good-humour with which he had entered his house. Had Dick been aware of this circumstance, he would, no doubt, have made his visit an hour or two later: for, young and inexperienced as he was, he nevertheless knew that the hour of ill-humour is not the hour for conferring favors. But chance so directed matters, that poor Dick came to the door at the critical moment when Mr. Harvey was in his very worst mood.

As, with throbbing heart, he entered the house, the first object that presented itself to his view, was Mr. Harvey, whose flushed cheeks and knitted brows immediately caught the youth's attention. Not more terrified is the defenceless lamb at sight of the angry lion, than was Dick at the sight of Mr. Harvey—so altered from what he had seen him a few hours before!—A simple refusal he could have borne, though not without sore regret, yet with a tolerable share of patience and resignation: but, for such a storm of unexpected anger as he now saw ready to burst upon his head, he was wholly unprepared. From the friendly mildness and liberality of Mr. Harvey's behaviour to him in the forenoon, he had every reason to expect at least a civil and quiet reception, whatever the final result might be:—how severe, then, the shock which he felt, when, by a sudden and un-accountable reverse, he now saw that gentleman's frowns and agitation threaten him with a harsh and stern refusal! His hopes and his fortitude at once forsook him: his heart shrunk within his bosom; his knees tottered beneath the weight of his trembling frame; and, from the deadly paleness of his countenance, he seemed on the point of sinking senseless to the floor.

A few moments previous to Dick's arrival, Mr. Harvey had been engaged in a scuffle. His head clerk, after having absented himself from his duty in the compting-house* during the whole preceding part of the day, had made his appearance there in the afternoon, quite drunk. Had his drunkenness been of the quiet peaceable kind, no material inconvenience would have ensued: but, unfortunately, he was one of those weak-headed mortals whom an extra glass works up to ungovernable fury.—Not content with insulting the other clerks, and tossing the books and papers about the floor, he was proceeding to break the windows, and commit still further outrages, when Mr. Harvey, having ineffectually endeavoured to pacify him or get him quietly out of the place, was at length obliged to employ violence, and, after considerable exertion, succeeded in thrusting him out by main force.

This scuffle it was, which had wrought so striking a change in Mr. Harvey's countenance, and, by its consequences, struck such a terror to the soul of poor Dick. But, the moment the youth made his appearance, that gentleman's features brightened up with a good-natured smile: instead of the fierce gleams of anger, the mild rays of benevolence now beamed from his eye; and he addressed the trembling orphan in a tone and manner which instantly banished all his late alarms, and cheered his drooping heart with the almost certain expectation of a favorable answer.

"Young man," said Mr. Harvey, "I am so far satisfied with the account I have received from the captain and passengers, that I am determined at least to make trial of you; and, as you now do 'see a probability of repaying the debt,' you may safely take some money in advance, to provide yourself with necessaries. I will send one of my clerks with you to purchase them, and provide you with a proper lodging; after which, you may enter upon your employment in my compting-house to-morrow morning, on a salary of a hundred and sixty dollars for the first year—to be afterward increased, if you justify my expectations."

Dick thanked him for his kindness, accepted the seasonable offer of pecuniary aid, and set out, as happy as a king, in company with the clerk, who assisted him in making the necessary purchases to the best advantage, and hired for him an apartment in a respectable boarding-house, after having discharged the mean lodging which he had taken on his first arrival.

Here we now behold Dick, within less than eight-and-forty hours after his arrival in New York, new dressed from head to foot, having spare money in his pocket, a decent room and a good bed to sleep in, with the certainty of a comfortable subsistence so long as he behaved himself properly: for, though a hundred and sixty dollars (which are only thirty-six pounds sterling)* would not go far in maintaining a person in London; yet, in America, where living was at that time so much cheaper, a young man, even of superior rank to Dick, might live pretty tolerably upon that sum. At all events, to *him* it was quite a fortune; and he owed it all (under the divine providence) to the diligence with which he had attended to his learning.

We need not doubt, that, when he retired to his room for the night, he kneeled down in grateful thanksgiving to that kind father of the universe, who had so providentially interfered in his favor. Harry Johnson, too, though born to better prospects than Dick, would have been thankful to God, devoutly thankful, if any person had made him such an offer, while he stood weeping over his mother's grave.

Harry, however, was not entirely neglected, or left to perish with hunger. Mr. Martin—the clergyman, whose notice he had so forcibly attracted during the funeral service at his mother's burial—after having learned the particulars of his distressful case, took him home to his own house, treated him with a good dinner, and endeavoured to cheer his spirits with the hope of better fortune; at the same time assuring him, that, if it lay in his power to render him service, he would do it with the greatest pleasure.

But Mr. Martin, however humane and charitable, had it not in his power personally to afford him any material assistance: for, in that country, the incomes of the clergy are very moderate; and, though Mr. Martin could, with economy, maintain himself and his family, and make, on the whole, a decent appearance, he had nothing to spare. The only mode, therefore, in which he could hope to render him any important service, was that of giving him his advice, and endeavouring to procure for him some situation, in which he might be enabled to earn his bread.

Having understood from Harry that he had been several years under the tuition of a Latin master and a French teacher, who had both regularly attended to give him lessons every day, it immediately occurred to him that Harry might be a very desirable acquisition to a friend of his, Mr. Stanmore, a member of congress, who wished to procure a tutor for his son, then about eight years old.

The good clergyman was delighted at the idea of having at once hit upon a plan which should mutually serve both parties; and he instantly imparted his thoughts on the subject to his youthful guest—taking for granted, that, with, *such* advantages of education, he *must* be capable of teaching a child of that age. Yet, before he would apply to Mr. Stanmore, he thought it right to examine Harry a little, for the purpose of ascertaining how far he was qualified to undertake the task. He accordingly put a few questions to him: but how great was his astonishment and vexation, upon discovering that the youth was wholly un-acquainted even with the first rudiments of grammar!

In the first moments of disappointment and surprise, he suspected that the account which Harry had given of his former condition in life, and particularly of his education, was only a tale of falsehood, artfully fabricated for the purpose of exciting compassion—and that he was *not* the son of a gentleman, but some low-bred, lying blackguard, who had perhaps been transported for thieving or picking pockets. Yet, on further consideration, the delicacy of Harry's complexion, together with the neatness of his clothes and the fineness of his linen—but more particularly the circumstance of his having come from England under the protection of that mother, whose loss he had heard him so bitterly deplore—induced him at length to believe that he was *not* a transported thief or pick-pocket, but actually the son of a gentleman, though he had unfortunately neglected to acquire that knowledge which would have proved him to be such.

But, though convinced of the truth of his story, Mr. Martin saw no possibility of serving him in the way he had proposed; and he was now sorry that he had mentioned Mr. Stanmore to him at all, as the disappointment of the hopes which he had thus raised, only served to depress poor Harry's spirits lower. Still determined, however, to serve the distressed youth if he could, he next recollected a merchant who wanted an under clerk: and "Surely," thought he within his own mind, "this young man must know enough of writing and arithmetic for that employment." Upon trial, nevertheless, he found that Harry wrote so wretched a scrawl, and had so little knowledge of figures, that he could not, with a safe conscience, or with any regard to his own character for veracity, venture to recommend him, even as an under clerk.

Some days now elapsed—days of cruel anxiety and alarm to poor Harry—during which the good clergyman exerted himself to the utmost of his power, to find some decent and comfortable situation for the forlorn orphan, whom in the mean time he every day entertained at his table with a plain, but wholesome and plentiful, dinner.

There were, it is true, several persons who would very willingly have taken him into their houses, for the purpose of running on errands, cleaning knives, blacking shoes, and performing various other kinds of mean, debasing drudgery; so that he was secure, at least, from the danger of actually starving, provided he were only willing to work, and render himself useful to his employer. But Mr. Martin aimed at something better for poor Harry, if there were any possibility of attaining it, and therefore would not immediately suffer him to accept any of those degrading offers—thinking it would be time enough to descend to them, if nothing more eligible could be found on further inquiry.

In his inquiries he was indefatigable: but the only situations he could hear of, above that of a servant to scour knives and clean shoes, were two—Mr.

Oakley, a neighbouring carpenter, and another person of a different trade, both wanted apprentices; and either of them would have taken a lad of Harry's age without an apprentice-fee.*

In his own mind, Mr. Martin gave the preference to Mr. Oakley, because *his* business was more lucrative than that of the other tradesman, and likewise more eligible in other respects. To him, therefore, he applied: but, at the very first sight of Harry—so thin, so slim, so puny, so feeble—the carpenter bluntly told the clergyman that "such a washy, water-gruel, smock-faced* Miss Molly* as *that*" (scornfully pointing at the poor fellow) "would not at all suit him; for that he never would be able to handle his tools, and would cost him more money for medicines, caudles,* and other slops,* in a single month, than he could earn in a whole year."

Harry's mortification and grief were now extreme: he regretted—deeply and bitterly regretted—that he had not attended to his learning. If he had, instead of being contemptuously rejected by a mechanic, he would have been gladly welcomed into the family of a member of congress, to sit down with him every day to a plentiful table, and ride out on a good horse with his son. His regret, however, was un-availing: it was impossible to recall the time past; and something must be immediately done, to save him from starving: for, though the humane Mr. Martin had hitherto entertained him every day, he could not afford to continue his hospitality for any great length of time—much less, to pay for his lodging and washing.

Seeing, therefore, that nothing more eligible could be devised, the good man applied to Mr Dapperly, the other person who was in want of an apprentice.—*He* did not object to Harry's slimness, because *his* trade did not require bodily strength so much as personal agility, and lightness of hand; therefore he agreed to take him as his apprentice, without any fee.

Sorely as Harry felt his pride wounded by the degradation of being apprenticed to a mean trade, yet the fear of either starving or blacking shoes induced him, however reluctant, to acquiesce in this arrangement; and he was accordingly bound,* in due form, by the overseers of the poor, as he had neither parent nor guardian in America, to deliver him over to his master.— Mr. Dapperly took him home, and began, next morning, to teach him his trade, which was that of a—— barber!

What a fall for poor Harry—brought up with the expectation of inheriting ten thousand a year, and occupying a seat in the British parliament—but now reduced, for bread, to shave the beard of every low plebeian who chose to pay a few pence for the use of his rasor!—a melancholy reverse, entirely caused by his own fault—by his obstinate and sinful neglect of the opportunities which had been offered to him during his father's prosperity.

He would now willingly have made amends for past neglect, and studied arithmetic, Latin, French, &c. to qualify himself for something more respectable than the lather-brush and rasor, at the expiration of his apprenticeship. But his wish was vain; for he neither had books, nor money to purchase them; neither could he have found time for study, unless he had stolen it from the hours of sleep. Besides, even if he had enjoyed both books and leisure, he knew so little, that he could not have proceeded a single step without the assistance of a master; and, in *his* situation, it was now utterly impossible for him to procure that aid.—A barber, therefore, he must remain, without any hope of ever bettering his condition.

Severe as was his mortification at this sad reverse of fortune, and the hopeless prospect before him, it would have been rendered still more severe by the contrast, if he had known, that, while *he* was lathering plebeians' beards, Dick Hobson, the son of his father's herdsman, was now, in comparison with him, quite a gentleman, and in easy circumstances.

Dick, indeed, had conducted himself so well, and given such satisfaction by his abilities and assiduity, that, before the end of the first six months, Mr. Harvey took him to board and lodge in his own house, without deducting a single dollar from his salary.—At the expiration of the year, the drunken clerk, whose misconduct had, on a former occasion, caused poor Dick so dreadful an alarm—but who, as it was his first fault, had then been pardoned on making a proper apology—was at length dismissed for repeated acts of ebriety* and neglect; and Dick, being charged with the care of the books which that clerk had kept, discovered various errors in the accompts, by which Mr, Harvey would have lost several thousand dollars.—Pleased with the discovery, that gentleman made Dick a present of fifty guineas, immediately doubled his salary, and promised to increase it still further after the lapse of another twelve-month. In short, after several successive increases of salary, Dick was finally admitted, at the end of five years, as a partner in Mr. Harvey's business; and the mercantile transactions of the house were thenceforward carried on under the united names of Messrs. Harvey and Hopson— for so the latter now wrote his name, to accommodate it to the delicate organs of the genteel company with whom he was accustomed to associate.*

Within less than eighteen months after his admission into the partnership, Mr Harvey gave him his daughter in marriage, with a very handsome portion: and Mr. Hopson, as we must henceforth call him, now enjoyed a fair prospect of making a rapid and immense fortune. His commercial dealings were extensive: and, as he exerted uncommon diligence in the execution of his plans, which were formed with consummate judgement, he was blessed with good success in every enterprise. In one of those mercantile adventures, having occasion to visit Pennsylvania about the time when Harry's apprenticeship was nearly expired, he arrived there on an excellent horse of his own, attended by a servant equally well mounted, who carried his master's great cloak and portmanteau.*

It was not from motives of parsimonious economy that he chose this mode of traveling: for, in his present circumstances, he was both able and willing to pay for every comfort and accommodation on his journey, which the country was capable of furnishing. But, luxury not having yet made sufficient progress in America, he could not there, as in England, command the convenient services of a hired post-chaise:* and, although there were stages,* which would, in sixteen or seventeen hours, have conveyed him from New York to Philadelphia, he chose to avoid the severe jolting which he must have suffered on the rough rocky road through the Jerseys,* together with the other inconveniences of those clumsy, awkward, uncomfortable vehicles, which better deserve the name of waggons than of coaches†. For these reasons it was, that he had preferred to travel on horseback, according to the almost general custom of every man in America who can conveniently keep a horse.

During his stay at Philadelphia, his servant happening to fall sick, and being unable to shave his master, as usual—Mr. Hopson was obliged to send out for a barber, to perform that office for him: and, as chance directed, who should that barber be, but Harry Johnson!—Had Mr. Hopson known him, he would certainly have exerted himself to better his condition, through gratitude for the memory of that worthy man whom his father had so often and so warmly praised to him as a most excellent master. But, as he had himself quitted England before Mr Johnson, and never heard of that gentleman's voyage to Philadelphia, he had not the most distant idea of meeting his son in America: and, though he had often seen Harry, and been formerly well acquainted with his person, it was impossible that he should recognise him in his present state—so pale, so wan, so meagre was he grown.

Without knowing him, however, he generously gave him a few pence for himself, in addition to the usual price of shaving, which he was to carry home to his master: and Harry, whose high spirit was now completely broken and debased by the habitual meanness of his condition—little suspecting that the scanty boon was bestowed on him by the son of his father's

† Indeed they are as frequently called *waggons* as *coaches*, particularly in those parts of the United States which contain many families of German or Low-Dutch origin; the same word, with them, equally signifying a *waggon* or a *coach*, viz. *wagen* in the German language, and *waegen* in the Low-Dutch.

THE BARBER !!

From *Learning better than House and Land* (2nd ed.; London, 1810)

cow-herd—received it with as lowly gratitude, as ever the cowherd's son had testified in his boyish days, on receiving a trifle from a gentleman, for holding his horse, or opening to him a gate.

IT is much to be regretted that the original manuscript record, from which this account of Harry and Dick has been compiled, does not contain any further particulars of their history. But, from every circumstance and every appearance, there is strong reason to conclude, that, if they be yet alive, Harry Johnson has not, to this hour, risen a single degree above the mean condition of a barber; and that Mr. Hopson, now possessed of immense riches, lives in affluence and splendor, honorably enjoying the fruits of his well-applied talents and indefatigable industry.—The difference of their fate suggests many important reflexions, which deserve to be seriously weighed by every young gentleman who feels an antipathy to his book: but, as they will naturally occur to himself, and I wish to save time and paper, I shall only copy out, for his perusal, the two following lines, with which the manuscript concludes—

"Whene'er a dislike to your learning you harbour,
Remember the fate of the gentleman barber".*

THE COMPILER.

P.S. In my preface, I promised to add a few remarks on certain passages of the narrative, relating facts in natural history or philosophy—the episodes of the shark, the porpoise, the rainbows, and the corked bottle—that the youthful reader may know upon what authority he is to rest his belief of the particulars. I now proceed to inform him, that I have myself seen the beautiful phænomenon of the fleeting rainbows, exactly as described in a preceding page.—I never saw it, except on one occasion: but it is sufficiently known to navigators; and, however clumsily or unphilosophically I may have attempted to account for it, the fact itself stands beyond the reach of doubt.

I have myself tried the experiment of the corked bottle; pursuing the same process, and producing the same result, as the reader has already seen. I made, however, a bungling business of it, by beginning at the wrong end, and sinking the bottle to so great a depth in the first instance.—I was preparing to correct my error: but, before the bottle could again be got ready, a breeze springing up prevented a repetition of the experiment; and I never afterward, during the passage, had another convenient opportunity, as it cannot well be made while the ship is under way.—Should any of my youthful readers ever be disposed to try it, let him at first sink the bottle only to a moderate depth, which he may afterward increase in successive trials, fathom by fathom, without the trouble of preparing the bottle more than once, until he shall have exactly ascertained the smallest depth at which the water possesses that amazing power.

Of the shark's rapacity and stupidity I have myself been an eye-witness. I have seen one and the same shark three times hooked and torn—seen his blood flow each time—seen him, after all this, return a fourth time to the bait, and swallow it—without having been one moment out of my sight during the whole transaction.—I saw two pieces of pork, which were taken from his maw in exactly the same state as those described in the history.— With respect to the discovery of the watch, though *I* never witnessed such an occurrence, yet the circumstance is not a fiction; at least it is no fiction of mine; for, in Dodsley's Annual Register, vol. 29, page 227, we have an account of a shark, taken in the Thames near Poplar,* in whose maw was found a watch, afterward recognised by a father, as the property of his son, who had been lost at sea two years before.*—I have seen shark's flesh served up at the captain's table on shipboard, and likewise seen a shark exposed for sale in the market-place at Oporto.

The strength and agility of the porpoise are not at all exaggerated. I have myself seen one of those fishes struck in the same manner as described in the history, and in the same manner escaping.—I saw the bent harpoon: I saw a piece of the poor creature's entrails sticking on the barbs; and I heard his assailant, a tall robust man, complain for some days of a soreness in his arm and shoulder, from the shock he had received on the occasion.—As to the fleetness of the porpoise, the calculation of his speed is entirely matter of conjecture: it may be over-rated or under-rated; and therefore the youthful reader is cautioned against adopting a supposition as a fact. This, however, he may safely believe, that I have myself watched, for near two hours, a shoal of porpoises that accompanied our ship in exactly the same manner as related in the preceding pages, while we continued sailing before a fine breeze at the rate of full ten knots an hour.

On the nocturnal mortality among the fowls, I cannot speak with equal confidence as on the other points: for, though I have, in more than one voyage, been a sufferer by those nightly deaths, I never could discover the cause—for want, perhaps, of having such a man as Thomas Hobson among the steerage passengers. I have, indeed, been subsequently *informed*, and by a seaman too, that the fact was as Thomas represented it; and even the mode was described to me, in which fowls are killed without noise or violence— the same which is said to be practised by the robbers of hen-roosts on land. All this, however, being only hearsay, I do not pretend to vouch for the truth of it, which therefore must, in the present case, entirely rest on the authority of Thomas Hobson, who made the discovery.—Neither can I vouch for the good consequences which are said to have resulted from the expedient adopted by Mr. Green and his fellow passengers, because I never saw it tried; though I doubt not, that, if it *were* tried, it would be productive of pleasing effects.

J. C.

THE END

Stories of Old Daniel

Frontispiece from *Stories of Old Daniel* (London, 1808)

STORIES

OF

OLD DANIEL:

OR

TALES

OF

WONDER AND DELIGHT.

LONDON:

PRINTED FOR THE PROPRIETORS OF THE
JUVENILE LIBRARY, NO. 41 SKINNER-
STREET, SNOW-HILL.

———

1808.

PREFACE.

THE greater number of the following stories were written with a view to indulge that love of the wonderful so natural to children of all ages and dispositions, without distorting their young minds by any thing too horrible or unnatural.

That there was such a person as Old Daniel' and that he amused the children of the village where he lived in this manner is perfectly true, but I have thought it expedient to suppress some of his stories, to alter others, and to supply him with several which he never heard of. I have also taken the liberty of making great improvements in his mode of expression, as I do not perceive any advantage children can derive from an acquaintance with vulgar or provincial phrases,' especially as it is not to be supposed they are capable of distinguishing what are fit to be adopted, and what ought to be avoided. When Daniel's diction is only simple, and not absolutely improper, I have endeavoured to preserve it, as it sometimes renders his narrations more interesting. Of these stories, some founded on facts are that of the *Bog-Trotter*, of the *Fortunate Reproof*, of the *Little Pedlar*, of the *Bears*, and of the *Little Boy who was Forgot at School*.

My great object in publishing these tales is to encourage in children a love of reading, which by becoming habitual may lead to profitable studies in their riper years: and as I have observed that among the great number of books for young people, there are comparatively few which attempt to turn the thoughts of their readers to foreign countries, and thus induce them to profit by the many well-written books of travels we possess, I have been rather desirous to give to my little stories this kind of novelty. I have endeavoured to afford my young readers (to borrow the words of a simple and elegant writer [†]) "little foretastes of the great pleasure which awaits them in their elder years," when circumstances may actually lead them to foreign lands, or a desire of knowledge turn their attention to the perusal of what travellers have written.

In short, my ardent wish is to promote as much as possible that love of literature, which procures *the most independent of all employments, and the most durable of all pleasures.*

† Charles Lamb: See Preface to Tales from Shakespear.

CONTENTS

STORIES

OF

OLD DANIEL.

CHAPTER I.

INTRODUCTION.

IN a little village, where I spent some of my earliest and happiest days, dwelt an old man whose name was Daniel. He was between ninety and a hundred years of age, but strong and healthy, retained his memory quite perfect, and related clearly many of the adventures of his youth. The neighbours were all kind to him: but their children doated* on him, for he used to tell them stories, and give them apples and gingerbread when they gathered about him; and many a wonderful tale had he of foreign lands and past days. He was always dressed in a brown great coat which buttoned down to his knees, and never was seen outside his door without an immense stick, which he boasted of using both as a support and defence. The little hair remaining on the back of his head was as white as snow, and his long beard (the most remarkable thing in his appearance) was of the same hue. His complexion was generally pale; but he had once been a soldier, and when he talked of battles, his cheeks glowed, and his eyes sparkled, as if his youth were renewed. In his walks he was constantly accompanied by a dog, who was almost as great a favourite with the village children as himself; and when he sat at home in his elbow chair,* his tortoise-shell cat always took her place at his feet. He had also a starling which imitated every sound that he heard: in fine weather his cage used to be hung up outside the window; and many a beating he occasioned to the little boys who stopped to talk to him on their way to school, until his master (being informed of the mischief he did) removed him to the other side of the house; however on Sundays and holidays the starling always appeared in his old place and every one was rejoiced to see him.

Daniel's cottage was one of the prettiest in the village: the white walls were almost covered with jessamine* and woodbine, which formed a porch over the door; and here it was that the old man used to place his wicker chair of a Sunday evening. Before the house was a green: in the midst stood a large oak, and beyond it ran a little stream, proceeding from a spring hard by, which never failed in the hottest days of summer. Behind his dwelling Daniel had a garden, where he still worked with his own hands; and in that garden stood the apple-trees from which he regaled his young friends: but none of them were ever allowed to enter it; for he used to say that if they were to run and play there as they did on the green, they must destroy the produce of his labour, and he could not bear to see them happy by halves. The thick privet hedge which surrounded this spot of ground was considered as an impenetrable wall. Many a wishful eye was cast at the fine apples, but Daniel's fruit was never stolen, and he often boasted, that in the course of thirty years his garden had never been robbed but once. The only person who lived with him was a poor deaf woman about sixty years of age, old Susan, whom he always treated as a child, because she was his own daughter, and having lived with him from her birth, he never thought of changing his method of treating her.

CHAPTER II.

THE CHURCH-YARD.

I WAS one of the flock of children that gathered at his cottage door of a Sunday evening to listen to his stories and partake of his fruit, which gave me so much pleasure that I wish now (at the distance of forty years) to impart it to my young friends; and as I cannot share the apples among them, I must content myself with telling some of the stories. The first time I recollect joining the village throng, was in the latter end of the month of August: my father had come to settle in the neighbourhood about a week before, and I well remember going to school for the first time on a Wednesday morning. As we were returning home on Saturday evening, I heard the little boys saying to each other, that they should meet as usual the next afternoon, and that Mr. Daniel had promised them a fine story and some choice apples. This raised my curiosity; and I soon found means to inform myself of the Sunday's amusement, and to be of the party.

As soon as the old man saw us, he singled me out as a stranger, asked my name, my age, from whence my family came, and many other questions of that sort: he stroked my head, said he was sure I should be a good boy, for my grandfather had been a brave officer, and then (turning to the rest) asked which he should give first, the story, or the apples. Some cried "the story," and some "the apples;" but he settled the difference by bringing out a basket of fine ripe apples; and, giving one to each of us, saying, "you may eat and listen at the same time," he thus began his story.

I WAS once quartered in a little village, where there was a church-yard, in which all who died within five miles round were buried; in fact such numbers had been interred there, that the ground was full of bones, and a new grave was never dug, without quantities of these being thrown up, so that the ground was strewed with skulls which were whitened by the air. Many strange stories were told of this same church-yard; and several of the old people who lived in that neighbourhood, talked of things that had been seen, and noises that had been heard, by those who happened to pass that way by night. The landlord of the public house where I (with two of my companions) lodged, was a very sociable, good sort of man; and as we were quiet lads, he often invited us into his parlour of a Sunday evening, that we might take our bowl of punch together. One frosty night we were sitting round his fire chatting, and as is often the case on such occasions we began to talk on the subject of ghosts. First our landlord told a story of a haunted house where he had once lived, and then his wife told another of a spirit that she said had appeared to her grandmother: each person related some anecdote of this sort, and every one was more terrific than the last, till at length we all began to look behind us, and I, who certainly could have marched up to the mouth of an enemy's cannon, felt myself shudder. Our good landlord perceiving this, replenished the bowl of punch, and we soon recovered our spirits. From one extreme we got to the other; and when our terrors were quite over, we laughed heartily at each other for being afraid of ghosts, and all, except our landlady and her sister, seemed to agree that it was a mere joke. Our landlord's daughter, a comely girl of nineteen, was silent, till one of my comrades saying that he was sure she believed in the reality of such appearances, she answered very modestly, "As to their reality, I cannot pretend to know any thing about that, but I am not afraid of any such thing, as I am sure it could not hurt me." All the men except her father seemed to doubt her courage; but he said, "I am sure Nancy tells the simple truth, for mild as she looks, I never knew her frightened: from an infant she has always had more courage than any of my other children, and I know not how to account for it, except that she has been always more attentive in saying her prayers and going to church than the others." "However," said the young man who had been joking with her, "I will venture to lay a shilling that she would not dare at this moment to walk to the church-yard and bring one of the skulls here." "Done," cried her father: "so wrap your cloak about you, child, and go as fast as you can." Nancy set out very chearfully; and as soon as she was gone, the landlord proposed to me to go with him another way to the burial ground, and watch what she would do. We reached the place before her, and hid ourselves behind an old wall. We saw her walk boldly forward, and take a skull from a heap near us, but just as she was going away, I could not refrain from calling out in a hollow voice, "That is my head, do not take it away!" She started, looked round her for a moment, then threw down the skull, and took up another. I cried out again (endeavouring in vain to assume another tone); "That head is mine, let it alone!" "Nay now," said she, "you do not tell truth, for you certainly had not two heads;" and she carried off her prize. We reached the house just as she entered it, and had a great deal of laughing about our adventure. At last Nancy said to the young man who had laid the wager, "I have a great notion you would not have been so ready to go yourself to the church-yard, as you were to send me there; but if you have a mind to prove that you are not afraid, take one of these knives, and stick it in any part of the burial ground you please, and we shall see by that means to-morrow morning how far you ventured." He was ashamed to refuse, so wrapping himself in a large great coat of the landlord's, he walked hastily out of the house. It was so cold that no one felt inclined to follow him, and we gathered round the fire to wait his return. The church-yard was so near, that we judged it might take him about ten minutes to execute his purpose, for it was a fine star-light night, and the path quite straight; but when half an hour had passed, we began to wonder at his delay, and at length my comrade and I determined to go in search of him. We found the gate open, and our companion very near it, lying on the ground, to all appearance lifeless. On hearing our voices he appeared to revive, and in answer to our questions, said, that he had done what he had engaged to do, and was going away, when something pulled him back with such force that he fell to the ground; that he had attempted twice to get up again, but was always pulled back, and that in truth he was half dead with cold and terror. We helped him up, and in doing so discovered the cause of his fright; for in sticking the knife in the ground with some force, he had also stuck it through the great coat, and so fastened it to the ground that, every time he attempted to go away it appeared as if he was violently pulled back. We brought him home with us as pale as ashes, and when he was well recovered, you may suppose how we all laughed at him. This was a constant joke against him in the regiment, and he never could have been able to support the raillery of his comrades long; but fortunately for him, in about two months after we had a desperate engagement with the enemy, and this very man distinguished himself so much above the rest by his bravery that the story was never after mentioned. So you see what a foolish thing it is to pro-nounce a man is a coward for being once frightened. I have heard many sto-ries of ghosts, and always when I had an opportunity of enquiring into the truth, found them to be much like that which I acted behind the old wall, when I claimed the two heads.

Here the old man paused, and giving another apple to each of us, desired us to go and play on the green, which we did with great merriment, Daniel still sitting at his door, and seeming to enjoy our sports almost as much we did ourselves.

A few days after, I discovered that old Daniel had told this story, for the purpose of correcting a little boy of our party, who had been taught by a foolish maid-servant to be afraid of ghosts, fairies, and all those sort of things,* and whom the other boys were in the habit of laughing at, and calling "coward."

CHAPTER III.

THE ROBBERS' CAVE.

SOMETIMES, as we were going to school, Daniel would look out at his window and bid us Good morning, but never suffered any of us to stop and talk to him, "lest," he would say, "your master should have the same complaint to make of me that he had of the starling." However in the evening as we returned, he would often talk to us for a few minutes in fine weather, but never asked us into his house, or gave us any of his good things, except of a holiday. On Saturday, or the eve of any holiday, he never failed to remind us of the treat he had for next day, and really it seemed to give as much pleasure to the good old man, as to us.

The second time I saw him I remember particularly well, for the gloomy appearance of the morning threatened to prevent our visit to the green, and when we met on the way to church, we lamented to each other that we should hear no story if it rained. However just after we came from church, a thunder-storm began, which lasted about half an hour, and before the time of meeting, the sun shone as bright, and the country looked as cheerful as ever. You may suppose how glad all the little boys were. I should not forget to tell you there were twelve of us, the eldest of whom was thirteen and the youngest nine, so you see we were old enough to understand Daniel's stories very well.

This evening he produced a very handsome basket of gingerbread, which old Susan had bought the day before at a neighbouring fair, and after giving each of us his share, he thus began his story:

YOU must know, my father, who was a worthy clergyman, brought me up with a strict love of truth, and always told me that, it was an imprudent, as well as a wicked thing, to tell a falsehood. The story I am going to relate proves he was right. When I was a very young lad, and first went into the army,* I was sent with the regiment into a part of the country that was infested by a terrible gang of robbers, who laid waste the whole neighbourhood. In the day-time they concealed themselves in the near mountains, where there were several caves and ruined buildings well adapted to their purpose; but at night they used to issue from their hiding places, and plunder the farm-houses, the little villages, and even the gentlemen's houses that were not very well guarded. Frequently they would take away three or four sheep at a time, sometimes as many cows and bullocks, and pigs and poultry without number; in fact it was principally in this way they procured food. They used often to borrow the horses of their neighbours, that is to say, they took them out of the fields by night, and brought them back again a few days after in a very bad condition. No traveller could pass in the dark without being attacked by them, and the riches they had gathered by robbing on the highway, as well as by plundering houses, were said to be immense. Several times the inhabitants of the villages had joined the constables* in large parties, to go in search of these disturbers; but though they frequently saw one at a distance, who seemed placed to watch, and who fled away the moment they appeared, they never met with any number; until one fine summer's morning, that a large party went early to the mouth of a cave, where they had reason to suspect some of these men were concealed. One of the constables and a farmer, who were more courageous than the others, advanced first, and were instantly shot dead, which caused the rest to make their escape in great haste. This was the first time they had ever been known to murder any one; but there is little difference between condemning a man to starvation by taking all he has in the world, and killing him. However, to come to my own part of the story, it was the death of these two men that caused our regiment to be sent into that part of the country. Some of the old soldiers, who had served in war-time and fought against the French, considered it rather a disgraceful thing to be sent against common robbers; but I thought it was good fun, and was glad to go to a new place. I did not then know how glorious it was to fight for one's king and country. We were welcome visitors on this occasion, and there was no trouble in procuring us lodgings, as I have often seen since. Two or three of us were placed in each house, and every body was delighted to have our company. I thought it a fine thing to be so caressed, and was better pleased than ever at having insisted on going into a profession which seemed to make friends so easily. I knew little of the world at that time. The first order we received, was to search through the mountains, and examine all the caves and ruined castles in the neighbourhood; and this I assure you was to me a very entertaining service, especially as I did not know half the danger of it. We went into several caves where we were obliged to carry torches; and I never saw any thing more beautiful than the glittering of the spar and icicles that were in some of these. In one, which appeared less damp, and was more spacious than the rest, we found some chairs and a table, also the remains of a dinner, which seemed to have been a very good one, and to have been eaten very lately; but none of the eaters shewed themselves. One great prize which I found behind a large rock, I must not forget: it was a little bottle of excellent rum; a most welcome treasure in a hot day to thirteen tired soldiers, who had no liquor but some of the common bad spirits of the country. This cave we examined with particular attention, and went into many different rooms (if I may so call them), but without discovering any further traces of inhabitants. We continued this occupation for a fortnight, and some of us patroled the country all night, without making any discovery; but we did not mind the fatigue, for it was shared amongst so many, and besides we were eating and drinking well. We were in a plentiful country, and no one thought any thing too good for us: in truth, since our arrival, the robbers had ceased to appear, and the inhabitants were very well satisfied with the exchange. I chanced to lodge in the same house with a soldier of my own age, who had not been taught to hate a lie as much as I did, and who often used to laugh at me for my strictness on that subject. It happened one day, that he and I had got permission to go to a town at some little distance, to provide our-selves with necessaries which were not to be had in the village, and meeting some of our acquaintance (for part of the regiment was quartered there) we were tempted to stay rather too long, which obliged us to make great haste in returning. My companion, who was young and giddy like myself, pro-posed our taking a short cut by the mountain, which would bring us near one of the ruined castles, formerly supposed to be the haunt of robbers, but which we had searched a few days before without discovering any sign of them. It was growing dark as we drew near the place; but we had no fears, so we laughed and sung and told comical stories by way of passing the time, until we came just under the castle-wall, when a loud whistle suddenly drew our attention, and we saw a man close to us, who immediately ran away, and at the same time we heard the sound of a great many footsteps and voices under the arch which we were approaching. We had not on our uniforms, and my companion said to me softly, "Say you are not a soldier." "No, Tom," said I, "I will never tell a lie." I had scarcely spoken these words when we were seized by six men, who tied our hands behind us, and hur-ried us into the castle, where one man held a dim lanthorn*, while the others examined us, and I assure you we were in a sad fright. "Are you a soldier?" was the first question. I said yes; my comrade said no. After taking our bun-dles containing all our morning's purchases, and searching our pockets, where they found scarcely any thing, for which they gave us some hearty curses, they blindfolded and led us forward for a few minutes without speak-ing; then a voice said "stairs," and we immediately descended. I counted fifty steps, before I found myself on level ground again, and we had not walked many minutes before the same voice cried "up-stairs," and we mounted about twenty steps. I then heard a door open, and was dragged forward for a moment. The same voice said again, "stay there," and the door closed.

Here Daniel told us, that, as it was a long story, he should finish it another time, "for my little lads," said he, "you are young, and I am old: you ought to run about and take exercise, and I ought to rest myself." It was impossible to murmur at any thing the good man desired, but I believe no twelve little boys ever went to play so unwillingly. However we consoled ourselves with the certainty of hearing the rest at our next visit, and ran away to the oak tree, which was a very fine one, and had a seat round it, where we usually consulted what should be our amusement. This afternoon it was determined to play at "hunt the hare,'" and I was chosen "hare," but I was so taken up with the thoughts of Daniel's story, that I ran much slower than usual, and was soon caught, and all night I dreamt of the robbers' castle.

CHAPTER IV.

THE SAME CONTINUED.

YOU may imagine how we longed for the next holiday, which fortunately happened on Thursday, and how delighted we were on Wednesday evening, when, as we were passing by, Daniel looked out of his window, and said, "I hope you have not forgot me and my comrade in the robbers' castle." "O no, no," cried we all; "and," added the old man, "I have as fine a basket of apples as you have ever seen." He then shut his window, and we ran to our different homes.

The next morning at the usual hour we assembled, Daniel shared his apples, and then sat down in his wicker chair, with his dog at one side, and his cat at the other, whilst we stood in a sort of semi-circle before him.

I left off, said he, when the door was shut, and the unfortunate captives left, with their eyes blindfolded, and their hands tied behind their backs. As soon as I thought our conductor was gone, I called out, "Are you there, Tom?" "Aye, that I am," said he, "but for God's sake do not speak to me." "Why not?" said I. "Ask me to-morrow if we are alive," replied Tom, "and I will answer you, but now I will not speak another word." I attempted two or three times to make him talk, but all to no purpose; and he afterwards told me it was because he feared some of them might be listening, and hear me say something which should prove him to be a soldier. Thus we remained about half an hour, as well as I could guess the time in such an uncomfortable situation, scarcely expecting to escape with our lives, for the men we had seen were most wicked-looking fellows. At length the door opened, and the same voice which we had heard before, said the captain had sent for us. This person then led us out, through several passages, down several flights of stairs, up others, and then down again, till at length we came into a place, where I judged by the sounds that a number of people were carousing. A different voice from any I had yet heard, asked me, who I was, why I had passed that way, what regiment I belonged to, and many other questions of that sort; to all which I answered with perfect truth, for I well remembered my good father's instructions; and it was lucky for me on this occasion. After they had finished examining me, they put the same questions to my comrade, who began by telling a falsehood very boldly, but soon betrayed himself, and at length got so puzzled that he knew not what to answer. I was then asked whether he was my companion, whether he had gone out for the same purposes, and whether he had been with me all day, to which I replied with the same truth as before. We were next led to a distant part of the room, and ordered to sit down. I heard a number of people speaking in a low voice, and seeming to dispute, but I could not distinguish what they said, and I own I was very much frightened. However in a few minutes a person led me forward and the voice I had last heard, said again, "In two hours you shall be set at liberty, and, if you will promise never to betray any person you see here, you may get a good supper before you go." I made the promise very chearfully, for I supposed people who talked in this way could have no thoughts of murdering; and in a moment the bandage was taken from my eyes and my hands set at liberty. Then indeed I was astonished at what I saw. In the middle of a vaulted room, from the top of which hung a large lamp with a great many lights, was a long table, covered with all sorts of good things; and round it sat no less than thirty men, with the wives of five of them, and I afterwards discovered that it was to these women I owed my good supper. They helped me plentifully to their best food, filled me a large glass of wine, and invited me to join in their merriment; but I looked round for poor Tom in vain, and I could not enjoy any thing, untill I knew what was become of him. At last they perceived how uneasy I was, and guessing the cause, the captain (who sat at the head of the table, and had questioned us the last time) said, "Your friend is safe, and shall go away with you in two hours, but we are afraid to trust him because he tells lies. We are not, to be sure, very particular about that matter ourselves, but we have confidence in people who tell truth, and we think you will be likely to keep a promise, so we are willing to humour the women, who wished you to sup with us." When I heard my comrade was safe, I ate my supper very heartily, and was treated with great civility by all, though the greater number and even the females had a savage appearance. They were very merry, talked a vast deal of their exploits and the escapes they had had, and I found they were much too cunning for us, and had often been near us when we least imagined. One man recollected me, as being the person who had discovered the bottle of rum in the large cave, where it appeared that three or four of them had been hid during our search. I also learned that they immediately knew us to be soldiers by means of this man who recognized me, that their idea was that we belonged to a large party who were coming to attack them, and had been sent forward as spies, and that if I had not told who we were and where we had been in the honest manner I did, they would have put us both to death immediately: but they discovered by my answers that our passing that way was a mere accident, and knew we could do them no harm. I found by their talk, that many of them were smugglers, and that a small number had inhabited those mountains, many years before they became a terror to the neighbourhood. They did exactly as they had engaged; in two hours they brought my companion to me still blindfolded and tied; they put a handkerchief over my eyes, and after again leading us up stairs, and down stairs, and through several long passages, where we heard iron bars and bolts in abundance, they set us at liberty just outside the arch through which we had entered, giving us a pass-word in case of meeting with any of their comrades. When I told my adventures to poor Tom, who had sat in the dark with his hands tied all the time, he swore he would never tell a lie again while he lived, and certainly he never after laughed at me for telling truth. Next day, some troops were sent to search the old castle, and we were of the party, but no one was to be found, and it appeared to me that the vaults, staircases, and passages were much smaller and fewer than the night before; indeed, I had since an opportunity of hearing that they led us round and round, and up and down, on purpose to make it more difficult for us to find our way another time, and as to the large room where I had supped, we were not able to make it out. In a very short time the robbers found that this was no country for them to live in, and one of the smugglers betraying them some were taken and the rest dispersed. I shall tell you some other time how I met with one of them ten years after, who was not at all glad to see me; but you may be sure I did not betray him, and he showed how much obliged to me he was by doing me a great service. As to poor Tom (for I know you will like to hear what became of him), his head was taken off by a cannon-ball in Germany some years after. I should not forget to tell you, that the reason the robbers detained us two hours was that we might not give the alarm too soon.

Daniel now dismissed us, and we ran away to our oak as usual, where we talked over the story before we went to play, and agreed that it was a very foolish and cowardly thing ever to tell a falsehood, and that it was lucky for our old friend that he had been early taught to tell truth.

CHAPTER V.

THE BOG-TROTTER.

ON the following Sunday we met as usual, and received our accustomed entertainment. The apples being distributed, the old man took his seat, with his constant companions, Trusty and Puss, and we gathered round him. After considering for some time, and looking much graver than usual, he began as follows:

There is nothing I like better than to see children friendly to each other, and many an act of friendship is repaid when least expected. Among the various places that I have lived in during the early part of my life, I was once about a twelvemonth in a little village in the north of Ireland,* which I always think of with pleasure. The inhabitants were industrious, simple, and contented, and I had the good fortune to be a favourite with some of the best of them, with whom I spent many happy days. It does me good even now, when I recollect our merry meetings, and the pretty dress of the peasants, who were all engaged in the linen business.* Of a summer's evening, when their work was over, you might see the men in their white jackets and trowsers*, looking so clean, with their bright buckles, and large scissars hung round their necks by a white tape, or perhaps a ribbon the gift of a sweetheart; and the girls in their white gowns and cloaks, with gay ribbons in their caps; and they used to dance so merrily—it almost makes me young again to talk of those days. But to return to my story: among the many friends I had in that neighbourhood, was a weaver, who had a large family, and was happy in having very good children; but one in particular, his only son, was the favourite of every one who knew him. The ladies and gentlemen who lived near, used to take a great deal of notice of him, and more than once wished to take him and educate him entirely without any expense to his family; but his father could not bear to part with him, nor would he have liked to leave his parents. One circumstance I must not forget, because I am sure you will think it very comical. When he was but three years of age, a rich old lady (who I suppose was a little mad), offered to take him and breed him up in a way much above what his father could afford; and certainly her offer was very tempting; but she insisted that he should wear petticoats till he was thirteen,* and this put a stop to the plan entirely, for his father could not endure the idea of having the boy laughed at by all his acquaintance. As he grew up he was more and more liked. His schoolmaster loved him for his docility in learning, and his school-fellows for his good nature, whilst his modesty and obliging manners endeared him to all the neighbours. Before he was eleven years old he possessed quite a pretty library, that had been given him by different ladies and gentlemen; and often the bettermost sort of farmers would come of an evening to borrow some of William's nice books. When he was about twelve years of age, it happened that his father had occasion to go to a great fair at the next market-town, to which the shortest way was across a bog, which was a very dangerous place at night, and the scene of many accidents: for it was of a prodigious extent, and full of holes which a person who mistook the way was liable to fall into. Often have I joined parties, that have gone out in dark nights and bad weather, to show lights to travellers who had gone astray there, and dreadful sights I have seen. William's father crossed the bog of a morning in fine weather; but the next day, instead of returning early as he intended, he was detained by a neighbour, who promised to accompany and afterwards disappointed him, till it grew duskish; still, as he knew the shortest way over the bog, and had frequently gone the same road, he had no doubt of reaching home before it was quite dark. After having taken a second glass of whisky punch to raise his spirits, he set off with all speed, and had got past the middle of the bog very safely, when a violent storm came on suddenly: the wind blew, the rain beat, and no shelter was to be had. William's father knew the dangerous ground he trod, and advanced very slowly, in hopes of not losing his way. The storm however increased, the poor man's cloaths' were wet through, and every step he took he found himself in greater difficulty. What to do he knew not: the cold rain had chilled him to the heart; he had no hopes of being able to reach his home that night; and though he continued advancing, it was with the utmost caution and terror. The bright flashes of lightning at first served to show him the dangerous spots; but when those ceased, he had no longer any direction. At length quite weary with cold, hunger, and fright, he sat down on the wet ground, shivering from head to foot, and almost certain that if he remained there till morning it would be the death of him, as he had lately been subject to bad fevers. By this time the roaring of the storm had somewhat abated, and the poor man thought he heard some one calling at a great distance. He supposed it might be some traveller as unlucky as himself, and thought, if *he* was at home, the traveller should not want assistance. Again he heard the sound, and louder than before; then making an effort to raise himself, he distinguished a glimmering light far off; this gave him hope, and he watched it for a long time. Sometimes it appeared in one place; sometimes in another: at length he saw it approach, and resolving to endeavour to make himself heard, he was just going to hallo, when he heard his name distinctly called. Immediately he answered, but the wind blowing towards him, had little hope of being heard: however he took courage, and proceeded cautiously to that part where he saw the light. Again and again he heard his own name called, and at length was able to convince the person who had come in search of him that he was near. When he reached the man who had taken all this trouble, he was very much surprized to find, that instead of being one of his friends, it was a person whom he did not recollect ever to have seen before. The man, however, expressed great joy at having found him, refused the reward he promised him, and after making him take share of a dram he had brought in his pocket, accompanied him on his way home. William's father, somewhat revived by the cordial, and the hope of soon being by his comfortable fireside, began to chat to the stranger as they were going along, and asked him what had induced him to take so much trouble about a person who was nothing to him; to which the other replied, that to be sure he was a good man, and would be a great loss to his family, but however that was not his reason for coming out to look for him: but, said he, "The fact is, that I have an only child at the school that your boy goes to. The poor fellow was always a well-disposed, good-natured child, but so dull at his book, that I was obliged to take him away from two schools, because the masters said they could not teach him, and the boys did nothing but laugh at him. At last God Almighty put it into my head to send him to the school where your son is, and there as usual the masters found him stupid, and the boys began to make game of him, when your good lad took him in hand, and by teaching him a little at play-time and other leisure-hours, brought on the poor child so much, that he now learns as well as the common run of boys, and escapes being brow-beat as he used to be, which often made my heart and his mother's ache. Your son shall have my blessing as long as I live, and I would go the end of the world to save any one belonging to him. So when I heard people talk of your being expected to cross the bog to-night, and found it growing late and bad weather, I resolved to come and look for you, and though every one said you would never think of coming till to-morrow, I knew I could not rest in my bed while there was any chance of William's father being in want of help. And thank God I did go, to bring you home to him safe and sound." You may imagine, my little friends, how proud William's father was, and how happy William himself was, at meeting with such a reward for his good nature to his school-fellow. Had he joined in making game of the poor child, it is probable his father might have perished in the bog. Go now, children, said old Daniel, with more severity in his countenance than I had ever before observed, and endeavour to take example by young William, whose goodness of heart procured a friend for his father in time of need.

We went off to our oak-tree with less alacrity than usual, and looking very sheepish; for however we were amused by this story, we felt that it was intended as a reproof to us, and saw very clearly that our old friend had been informed of a circumstance that had caused great displeasure to our school-master. It was this; two little boys who had come to school after me were very dull; indeed it was scarcely possible to teach either of them; and we used to laugh at them and call them *Master A B C,* and *the Wisemen,* &c. which sadly discouraged the poor children. This story however had the desired effect, we left off making game of them; and to show how little is to be judged from the beginnings of children, the elder of these boys made a wonderful progress in arithmetic, and became a rich merchant; and the younger raised a fortune at the bar;* whilst I who used to ridicule their dull-ness was no better than a common soldier.

CHAPTER VI.

THE FORTUNATE REPROOF.

O N the next holiday we approached the house of our old friend with more timidity than usual (all except the poor boys whom we had used so ill), and recollecting the severity of his looks the last time we saw him, were very much afraid of finding an appearance of displeasure still remaining in his countenance; but we were soon relieved from these apprehensions, and made very happy, by seeing him look as kind as ever, and appear particularly glad to see us. He brought out a large basket of fine plums, and after sharing them very liberally among us, said, I have always a good opinion of children who mend their conduct on a slight reproof. I had last night the pleasure of a visit from my worthy friend your school-master, and he has given me a very satisfactory account of you. Talking of the benefit of slight reproofs, reminds me of a story I heard when I was in France, which I know to be true, as it was told to me by a near relation of the parties concerned.

A VERY respectable man in a learned profession had a son, to whom he wished to give the best education possible, and whose character he had studied with the utmost attention from his earliest years, nourishing with care his numerous good qualities, cultivating his talents, and gently correcting the faults which usually accompany genius and sensibility. At the age of fifteen this youth had made an uncommon progress in his studies, and his father, who intended him for his own profession, flattered himself that his own celebrity would be augmented by that of his son. The young man attended his college regularly every day, but always returned at night to the house of his father, where he used to sup with the family, and enliven that social hour by the acuteness of his remarks and the brilliancy of his wit. Gaming was the predominant vice of the town where he lived, and it happened that in the way to the college was a billiard-table, which proved very attractive to many young people of that neighbourhood. Several times in passing by Louis had cast a wishful eye at this place of amusement; he felt a great desire to join in the diversion, but he recollected the particular aversion his father had to all sorts of gaming,* and pursued his way: but the oftener he passed, the stronger became his wishes to join the party, and at length in an unlucky hour he was tempted to forget his father's precepts and his own good resolutions. This occurred at a most critical time; for a public examination was to take place very soon, and all the young lads who had any hopes of being distinguished were studying with particular attention: Louis was among this number; and the opinion entertained of his talents by his tutor and parents was such, that they expected the highest honours would fall to his lot on this interesting occasion. Unfortunately it was at this moment that he was seized with the spirit of gaming, and instead of devoting his days to his studies, he spent half his time in the billiard-room. His tutor was much surprised at his negligence, and began to fear he had lost that ambition which had hitherto urged him to make such progress. At length, three days before the examination was to take place, a friend of his father's, passing by, perceived the unworthy manner in which the ingenious youth was occupied, and after remonstrating first in gentle and then in severe terms, at last went so far as to threaten to inform his father of his conduct. This roused the indignation of Louis; and treating his threats with the utmost contempt, he continued his pursuit with such ardour, that after losing all his money, he was stripped of his watch, shoe-buckles, and knee-buckles.* He then returned home very much ashamed of himself, recollecting how just had been the reproofs of his father's friend, and still hoping that he should be able to conceal his misconduct from that father whom he so highly reverenced. As it was later than usual when he reached his house, he flattered himself that he might escape to his room without being observed, and either find some excuse for not appearing at supper, or contrive by proper arrangements to conceal his losses. However, unluckily his father was standing at the door when he arrived, and asked where he had been so late, to which he made some sort of muttering reply, and wrapping his coat round him, endeavoured to pass up to his room; but his father stopped him; and after asking several questions about his studies, which extremely embarrassed him, as he had not been at his college that whole day, told him that supper had been some time on the table, and desired him to join the party who had already sat down. After making several excuses, and saying he had no appetite (which was perfectly true), he succeeded in escaping to his room, where after locking his door, he threw himself on the bed a prey to the most melancholy reflections. He thought of the folly of his conduct, of the time he had misspent, and the probability of his losing the expected premiums; which would be a still greater mortification to his parents than to himself. He sincerely repented of what he had done, and resolved that he would work day and night, to endeavour to gain those honours which he had scarcely a hope of attaining, as the examination was to take place in two days. However, he got up at the first dawn of morning, and continued at his books (scarcely allowing himself a moment to eat his breakfast) until the hour for going to college, when he hastened to his tutor's apartments, taking care to turn his head the other way as he passed the fatal billiard-room. He attempted to make some awkward excuse for his absence, but his master did not appear curious on the subject, and he pursued his studies all day with the greatest diligence. Being conscious of having done every thing in his power to make amends for his misconduct, he returned home in much better spirits than the night before, but by no means as cheerful as usual; for he was oppressed by the fear of his worthy father's discovering how ill he had behaved, and also by the dread of being disgraced at the examination: for Louis was an ambitious youth, and would have considered it a disgrace to have failed of meriting those distinctions, which a knowledge of his talents had led his friends and teachers to expect. As soon as supper was over, he hastened to his room, intending to sit up at his studies as long as he could keep his eyes open; but on approaching his table, how was he astonished to see his watch, his buckles, and a purse, containing at least as much as he had lost in his visits to the billiard-room! You may imagine what his feelings must have been on this occasion. He was too much ashamed and overcome by this new instance of paternal kindness (which at the same time he felt as the strongest reproof), to mention the matter to his father. His heart felt so truly grateful, that he had no words to express his thanks, and the delicacy of both parties was such, that they never spoke on the subject after; but Louis was for ever cured of his propensity to gaming, a vice to which his ardent temper and the example of his associates would have rendered him particularly liable. I should not forget to tell you that the youth's exertions were crowned with success; he carried off all the first prizes, and fulfilled the most sanguine expectations of his friends.

This story produced a different effect from some of the former: three or four of the boys thought it was the prettiest they had ever heard, and wished to hear a great deal more about Louis and his father, but the remainder did not think it half so entertaining as some of Daniel's former stories. I thought it very pretty, but to tell you the truth I liked the story of the robbers' castle much better.

CHAPTER VII.

FATHER GIACOMO.

THE next Sunday turned out very wet, and we were obliged to give up all hopes of our customary amusement. The rain would not allow of our assembling at Daniel's door, and his house was not large enough to contain half our number with convenience. This was a sad disappointment; but our old friend took care to tell us from his window, as we passed by on Monday morning, that he should try to recollect one of his best stories for the next time; and luckily we had a half holiday to look forward to in the course of the week. The day proved remarkably fine, and we met rather earlier than usual. Daniel and all his companions appeared particularly glad to see us: Trusty wagged his tail, puss purred, the starling fluttered in his cage, and old deaf Susan, with a smile, produced a large supply of cakes and apples, which were divided in plentiful portions.

Well, my boys, said Daniel, I am happy that we have got a fine day again, and I have been considering what story I should tell you this evening. I promised you an account of my meeting, ten years afterwards, one of the men I had seen in the robbers' castle, and I do not recollect at this moment any story which I think could amuse you better.

YOU have often heard me say that I have travelled a great deal, and that I have been in many different situations in the course of my long life. I was once servant to a gentleman, to whom I was very much attached. He had been my officer: I had fought by his side, and once had the happiness of saving his life. God rest his soul: it is to his bounty I owe my present comfortable support. He was as generous a man, and as brave an officer, as ever gave the word of command.

When the war was over, he resolved to travel, in hopes of diverting his attention from some family misfortune, and offered to take me, rather as a companion, than a domestic. I was glad to go with him any where; so we set out together, and many a long mile we travelled, and many a strange adventure we had in our journeys.

One day, as we were passing through a little village in Italy, the carriage broke down; and as the people of that place work slowly, we were obliged to wait three days before it could be sufficiently repaired to convey us to the next great town. However as the accident happened in a romantic part of the country, and the weather was tolerably fine, my master (who had no particular object to hurry him) did not murmur at the delay, and we passed our time very agreeably in wandering about the neighbouring mountains.

On the third day, as we were entering the inn, a Franciscan friar was coming out, and met me so directly, that I could not help looking him full in the face, as he did me at the same moment. We both started, and he turned as pale as ashes. I was astonished to discover in him one of those whom I had particularly noticed in the robbers' castle: his was not a countenance to be easily forgotten. He had a long face, a sallow complexion, large aquiline nose, and small eyes as black as jet; his heavy black brows almost touched his eye-lids, and met over his nose; he was besides under-jawed, and had the mark of a large cut on his right cheek, which was a fresh wound when I first saw him. Notwithstanding the great alteration in his dress, I instantly recognised him, and was surprised to find by his countenance and manner, that he also recollected me immediately. He let fall an empty basket which he carried on his arm, and as he stooped to take it up, took an opportunity of pressing my foot in a very significant manner, and I understood his meaning. My master, who had observed me start, asked me, when the monk had passed, what was the cause, which I merely said, was the meeting this strange-looking man so suddenly; for I remembered the promise I had made so many years before, and saw it was of consequence that I should keep it. My master appeared to be almost as much struck with the uncommon appearance of the man as I was; and when the servant of the inn brought up the dinner, asked some questions about the monk he had met below stairs. She replied, that he was a very holy man who had made many pilgrimages; that he frequently came to this village, to collect alms for his convent which was at some distance, and to dispose of the produce of his garden; that he was a foreigner, she did not know exactly from what country; and had come a great many hundred miles from his native place to settle in Italy. When I went down stairs, I asked several other questions about this man, and was informed, that father Giacomo was quite a saint, that he had converted many sinners from their evil ways by his preaching, and that he had lately paid the greatest attention to two murderers who had been executed in that neighbourhood, had voluntarily assisted them day and night to the last moment, and had allowed no other spiritual aid to be called in. Every mouth was open in his praise, and some of the simple villagers even went so far as to think there was something holy in his looks.

In the evening, as we were waiting for the carriage, which had been promised to us hourly since the morning, I was astonished to see father Giacomo enter our apartment. He apologized politely for his intrusion, and said he came for the purpose of collecting money to be paid for certain prayers, customary to be said in that district at this season, and hoped we would be so kind as to contribute. My master, who always conformed himself to the usages of the country where he was, immediately gave him a small piece of money, and I did the same: he thanked us, and retired, but when he had reached the door, turned back, and looking at me, said in English, "People are often rewarded for their fidelity when they least expect it." He spoke this in such a foreign accent, that I believe my master did not think he perfectly understood the words made use of, and just as he was beginning to make some remarks on the singularity of the monk speaking our language, the person who had repaired the carriage came to be paid. The delays we had met with, and the weather having become unfavourable for our walks, made us very impatient to depart; and though we had heard much of banditti* which infested this part of the country, and were strongly advised by the inn-keeper to wait till next morning, my master was determined to set out immediately. Amongst the crowd that surrounded the inn-door as we were getting into the carriage, I observed father Giacomo, and looked back to salute him; but he seemed to be engaged in conversation, and took no notice of us.

The morning had been wet; but in the afternoon the day had cleared, and a short time after we left the village, the sun set in a most brilliant manner. The road which winded among the rocks was bad, and we went very slow, but whilst we had light to distinguish the surrounding scenery, our journey was very agreeable. At length it grew duskish, and whilst we were ascending a very long hill, my master (as was his custom) fell into a profound sleep, in one corner of the chaise,* whilst I composed myself in the other, and thought of all I had seen of my past adventures; the dangers I had been in; the hardships I had suffered; and, in short, all those things that are so agreeable to reflect on, when one is sitting at one's ease in a comfortable carriage, or by a snug fire-side. It was almost dark, when we entered a wood whose shade made the hour appear even later than it was, and I felt my reverie very much interrupted by the irregular manner in which the postillion* drove, at one time so slow, that I thought every instant he was going to stop, and in a minute after galloping on, as if he was running away from some one. Still my master continued to sleep sound, and I was very glad he was not disturbed: but at length, just as we came to a turn in the road, a number of men rushed from among the trees, and stopped the carriage. I at first thought of having recourse to our pistols, but immediately recollected how very foolish, and to how little purpose it would be to attempt opposing so many; and I had scarcely time to wake my master, and tell him what had happened, when both doors were opened, and we were dragged out of the carriage. Two of the men went on each side of the postillion, threatening him with their daggers, whilst he obeyed their commands in turning off the

road into an opening of the wood, and we were obliged to follow with similar attendants. Resistance was vain, our opponents were numerous, and our
postillion appeared to be quite panic-struck. We walked on very slowly for
a few minutes, indeed it was so dark that we could scarcely see our way; but
this did not prevent my observing a cross placed on one side of our path,
which marked the place where a murder had been committed, and you may
judge whether I shuddered at the sight of such an object at such a moment.
The banditti soon ordered the driver to stop, and taking the horses from the
carriage, very deliberately set about taking off our trunks, and ransacking the
inside of the chaise.

And now, my little friends, said old Daniel, as we have left them so busily
employed, you may go and play; for you know that I am not a very young
fellow, and cannot talk a long time without being tired. We were forced to
submit, for the old man had an imposing manner which admitted of no
remonstrance; but our curiosity was so great, that I am afraid we should not
have considered our good friend's fatigue, could we have found any means
to induce him to continue. However there was no remedy, and we ran off
to our usual sports.

CHAPTER VIII.

FATHER GIACOMO CONCLUDED.

I BELIEVE it is scarcely necessary for me to tell you with what impatience we expected the next holiday, nor with what satisfaction we saw the sun rise bright and beautiful on that morning. I can answer for myself, that I was much more impatient for the conclusion of this wonderful story, than for Daniel's good things; however I had no objection to the feast of fine plumbs and apples that our old friend had prepared, but was very glad when he continued his story as follows.

WHEN the robbers had completely removed every thing out of the chaise, they divided our luggage amongst four of the party, and advanced into the wood, leading us on in the same manner as before. I should not forget to mention, that they fastened the horses to a tree, and left them with the carriage. We had not proceeded far, when we came to a small building, the form of which it was too dark to distinguish. One of the banditti pulled a bell at the gate, which was opened in a few minutes by a venerable looking man in the dress of a hermit, whose beard was almost as long and white as mine is now. I was never more surprized, than when he gave his blessing to these ruffians, and received them as friends, but I soon found out what a sad old rogue he was. As soon as we had entered the building, he closed the gate, and locked it carefully, then led the way into a large room, where there was a long table and benches; and putting down his lamp, he gave a key to one of the banditti, and pointed to a door at the far end of the chamber: this man, who was a ferocious looking fellow, beckoned to us in a sort of authoritative manner, and led the way to the door, which he opened; my master, the postillion and I followed; he made a sign to us to go in, and then shut the door, perfect silence being preserved by all parties while this arrangement was making. As soon as the door was closed, the party in the outer room began to talk very earnestly; and seemed to be disputing about the proper place for depositing the booty; in the mean time we remained in dreadful suspence, the postillion assuring us that we had no chance of escaping with our lives, and in all the intervals of his prayers, which he repeated from time to time with great fervency, relating some of the horrid anecdotes of this wood, which had long been notorious for similar adventures.

At last the door opened, and the hermit entered accompanied by four men, armed with those sharp daggers called in Italy *stilettos.*. I do not think I ever beheld four such savage looking creatures; and you may imagine how we felt when one of them desired us to confess our sins to the hermit, who was ready to prepare us for death, as we were to die immediately. The unfortunate postillion instantly accepted the offer, and retiring to a corner of the room with the old villain, began to speak very earnestly in a low tone of voice. In the mean time the four murderers stood gazing at us, as if they were impatient to begin their cruel work. A single lamp, burning before a picture of the Virgin, threw sufficient light on the surrounding objects to show us all the horror of our situation, which the energetic whispers of the man who was preparing to die with us, rendered still more awful.

In this terrific moment a loud ringing and violent knocking at the outward gate was heard; the banditti started, and the hermit, leaving his penitent on his knees, hurried with them out of the chamber, not omitting however to lock the door on us. This respite inspired us with hope; and my master and I, arguing that any change in our situation must be for the better, endeavoured, but in vain, to encourage our unfortunate companion, who seemed not to have the slightest expectation of saving his life. After some time we heard a great bustle and a number of voices in the next room; in a few minutes the door opened, and father Giacomo met our astonished looks. He immediately turned to me, and said, "Had you betrayed me, I should have left you to your fate; you have been faithful, and I come to reward you." He then brought us into the outer-room, where we found nobody but the wicked old hermit, who looked very much humbled and disappointed. Our protector made us all sit down, and by his order the old hypocrite produced a bottle of excellent wine, which we partook of without ceremony, and then father Giacomo after calling for a lanthorn led the way out of this dreadful place, directing us to follow him, which you may be sure we did with the greatest alacrity. He led us out by a different way from that we had come, into the road, and there to our great surprize we found our baggage replaced on the carriage, the horses put to, and all ready for our departure. After lighting the lamps at father Giacomo's lanthorn, we bade him farewell, with a thousand expressions of gratitude; and just as we were setting off, he said to me, "Let this be a warning to you always to act honourably." In truth had I not done so, it is most probable we should all have perished; for this was a dreadful gang, and had committed various atrocities. How father Giacomo had acquired so much power over them I know not; but it did not last long after this, for in consequence of some act of violence to some great person in that country, the *Sbirri* or police-men were sent after them; and on our returning the same way six months after, we were told that seven and twenty of the gang had been taken, and that two or three priests who had been discovered to be connected with them, had been sent to their respective convents, to be punished by their superiors. I also heard it lamented that the good father Giacomo had left off visiting that town, but no one seemed to have the slightest suspicion of the cause.

That night we travelled about two hours, during which I amused my master, whose curiosity had been greatly raised by the monk's mysterious speeches, with an account of my adventures in the robbers' cave and castle, and a great many circumstances relative to them which I now forget. He praised my conduct very much, and said he was happy to travel with a man of honour.

Old Daniel asked us a few questions concerning our opinion of this story, and I remember particularly well that he was much pleased with my answers, and said he hoped I should be a soldier. He then dismissed us as usual to play on the green, and sat looking at our sports.

CHAPTER IX.

THE LITTLE PEDLAR.

THE week after this, a circumstance occurred in the village, which gave rise to much conversation amongst all classes of the inhabitants, and even came to be discussed in our little circle of boys. A young man who had left the town eight years before with only two guineas in the world, returned to settle at his native place with a large sum of money, and was looking out for a farm to buy, saying he could afford to lay out six or seven hundred pounds in the purchase. As he was of a reserved disposition, and did not take the trouble of telling his history to any one, the curiosity of all the neighbourhood was raised to a great height, and a thousand conjectures were immediately afloat. Some imagined he must have got his riches by a great prize in the lottery;* others were sure he had found a hidden treasure; but the greater number (I am sorry to say) were inclined to believe he had not come honestly by his money. At length the little boys began to talk the matter over, and as the greater number of us were destined to earn a livelihood by our industry, it was really very interesting to know, that Tom Hammond had left home with two guineas, and at the end of eight years had returned with more than seven hundred. I believe no set of little boys ever talked so much of such an affair before: we differed in opinion, and had great disputes relative to what sum might be necessary for beginning to make a fortune; some thought one guinea might be sufficient, others two, and others thought five would be little enough. At length we determined to refer the matter to our old friend, whom we all considered as the wisest man in the world.

On the next Sunday, the moment we saw him, we all began to ask his opinion, but in such haste and with so much confusion, that he ordered us, with an air of authority which he could well assume, but which we seldom saw, to let one speak for all, and beckoning to me, enquired what this great affair was. I told him I wanted to know how long he thought it ought to take a man, to make seven hundred guineas from two. He had already heard all that was said of Tom Hammond, and was not so much astonished at his success as his more ignorant neighbours. In reply to my question, he said, that he had seen too much of the world to surprized at our townsman's good fortune, at that it was impossible to tell what might be done by great diligence and industry, or to judge what any particular person was capable of; for that what was quite out of the power of one man, might be effected by another: to shew you, my children, added he, how these things are done, I will tell you a story of a little boy whom I happened to know. This also was in the north of Ireland.

Harry Millar was the son of a poor man who kept a little shop in a village where I was once quartered. Unfortunately his father was idle and drunken to the greatest degree; but his mother was one of the best women in the world: the most quiet, patient, industrious person I ever met with. She had received a very good education for a person in her station, that is to say, she could read, write, and cast accounts, better than any of her neighbours, and in fact it was she who took care of the shop. She used to sit all day behind the counter, with a bundle of old cloaths by her side, which she would mend at every leisure-moment, while her good-for-nothing husband was spending his money at the ale-house; when he was enquired for, she never told where he was unless it was absolutely necessary, and though there was every reason to suppose that when he returned drunk and out of humour, he used to beat the poor woman, she was never known to complain. She never talked to any one of her own affairs, and never encouraged any gossipping acquaintance.

Her greatest wish was to give little Harry (who was her only child) a good education; for of this she knew that no one could deprive him, and she had too much reason to fear, that his father, especially if she should die first, would soon make away with any money she might be able to save. Fortunately there was a very good, cheap school within an hundred yards of her house, and here she sent Harry every day, notwithstanding the murmurs of his drunken father, who said he did not see any use in the boy being as learned as the parish-clerk. He did not however interfere while he was able to pass his time with his idle companions; and his poor wife's whole anxiety was directed to little Harry. He was a fine smart boy, and made a rapid progress at school; and his mother, who had found in religion the greatest consolation of her life, took pains make her son as pious as herself. She taught him his prayers and catechism, and used to read passages out of the Bible to him of a Sunday evening. She explained to him the folly and wickedness of telling falsehoods, shewed him by her own example the benefit of being honest and taught him to depend on the protection of Heaven in all difficulties and dangers. Little Harry profited by all these good instructions; and at eleven years of age was the greatest comfort possible to his poor mother, whose health had become very bad. He could not love his father, whom he seldom saw, and then generally drunk; but he was taught to behave to him with respect and kindness, and to do every thing he could to serve him.

When Harry was about twelve years old, his mother, who had long been in a declining way, died after keeping her bed only two days; and in less than a week after, his father was carried off by an epidemic fever, which swept away numbers of the inhabitants of that place. Poor Harry was also very near dying, but at length he recovered, and as soon as he was able, set about enquiring what remained to support him after his father's goods, which had been seized by the creditors, were sold. When every one was paid, and all the debts attendant on their illness discharged, there remained for Harry only *sixteen-pence*; however he was not disheartened, and resolved to begin the world with this sum, "hoping with the help of God he should do very well." He had made such good use of the few years he was at school, that he could write and cypher better than many twice his age; and so, determining to keep an exact account of all his gains, he resolved to traffic with his fortune of *sixteen-pence*. For this purpose he walked to the next great town, and laid out his money in tobacco, which he sold in small quantities, with so much profit, that he doubled his capital in a short time; he then laid in a larger stock, and sold it in the same way; and as he never tried to impose on any one, and sold at the same price whether his customers were drunk or sober, he soon made a character for himself at the villages he was accustomed to frequent. During this time he had board and lodging at the house of a relation, who was scarcely able to give him even that assistance; but he looked forward to supporting himself entirely, and therefore was very diligent in his business. As his profits increased, he added a quantity of ballads* to his other merchandize, and by what he gained at two or three great fairs, was at length enabled to lay in a stock of knives, scissars, pencils, and such things as hardware pedlars usually carry; taking care at the same time always to have a good supply of tobacco, which he had found a most lucrative article of trade. He then ventured to travel to some distance, and in about a year after, I saw him at a town more than two hundred miles from his native place. Although he then possessed in money and goods near four guineas, he had met with some misfortunes, which he said had kept him down in the world. I asked him what sort of misfortunes, and he gave me an account of them.

The first happened about two months after he had left home, and was indeed a very alarming accident. As he was going to a gentleman's house, where he had before sold some of his hardware, and had been desired to return, he was met in the avenue by a dog running very fast, which bit his leg as he passed by. The wound was trifling, and he continued his way; but when he got to the hall-door, he found the servants in great consternation, on account of a mad dog which had just bit several animals about the house, and every one asked him if he had met it. He said he had met a dog a few minutes before, which had bit him, and shewed where his leg was bleeding. The alarm was immediately spread through the house, and a surgeon who happened to be there on a visit, cut out the piece of flesh, and seered it with a hot iron:* this the poor boy said was a very painful thing, but it was better than to go mad, and bite people, and die a miserable death. The master and mistress of this house were very good to him; they kept him there till he was quite recovered, and gave him half-a-crown when he was going away.

The other misfortune he seemed to think more vexatious, and besides it had made him wicked he said, which the mad dog's bite had not. At a little inn, in the suburbs of a great city, where he had gone to purchase some articles of trade, he had imprudently shown his purse, containing seventeen shillings, all the cash he had in the world, and while he was asleep some person had taken it out of his pocket. This put him into a violent passion, and he cursed and swore for the first time in his life (for his poor mother had often cautioned him against that wicked practice) and heartily wished he could see the thief hanged. However all this was to no purpose; all enquiries were in vain; and he was obliged to set off without it; thanking God however that his little merchandise had not been taken also.

This was a very extraordinary boy. By his answers to questions I put to him, I found that he kept a regular account of every halfpenny that he spent or received, and wrote it down every night before he went to bed; that he never by any accident neglected to say his prayers night and morning; that he washed himself, and combed his hair every day, and never failed to have a clean shirt to go to church in of a Sunday. I heard of him once, about a twelve-month after, that he was going on very well, had got a good deal of money, and had every reason to expect that he might make his fortune in a few years.

You see, my young friends, by this story, what may be done with diligence and industry, and I have known several instances of the same sort, though none equal to this, which is wonderful on account of the child's age, and the very small sum of money. You may suppose therefore that it is impossible for me to tell exactly the sum necessary for a man to make his fortune, or how many years two guineas would take to grow into seven hundred; but to me it does not appear so very strange for Tom Hammond to have made seven hundred pounds in eight years, and I think it more probable that he has acquired this property by diligence, than by any of the extraordinary means his neighbours are willing to suppose.

Here our old friend dismissed us, and we ran away to our oak-tree as usual, full of admiration for little Harry Millar, and not near so much inclined as before, to listen to what the talkative neighbours said of Tom Hammond.

CHAPTER X.

THE MAN-HATER.

OUR next Sunday's entertainment was interrupted by torrents of rain, and we were this time a whole fortnight without hearing one of our old friend's stories. I assure you we considered it quite as a misfortune, especially as the time was approaching, when we could no longer hope for this sort of out-a-door amusement: for Daniel had been in the habit of telling stories in this manner for several years, but always left off some time in the month of October which we had now entered.

The Sunday after turned out very dry, and though there was a white frost in the morning, yet at the hour we usually assembled it was by no means cold. Our good friend appeared particularly glad to see us, and so did all his companions: Trusty wagged his tail, Puss purred, the starling flapped his wings, and old deaf Susan, smiling, brought out a basket of very nice cakes, in addition to the customary treat of fruit.

Well, my lads, said Daniel, here is another fine Sunday for us, and I have had time to recollect, and chuse among my stories one that I hope will please you all. I know you like to hear of foreign countries, and so I have been thinking of my adventures abroad.

I WAS once travelling with my dear master in Germany about this time of the year. The weather was fine, but very cold, and the roads extremely bad; we got on slowly, and having been accustomed to the quick travelling in England and France, were made very impatient by the continual and causeless delays that now prolonged our journey. In consequence of this we used frequently to travel very late, and as there were no highway-robbers in that part of the country, we suffered no apprehensions except from the badness of the roads. One evening about seven o'clock we arrived at a little post-house' by the road-side, where, had we even wished to remain, there were no accommodations. After waiting some time, and receiving repeated assurances that the horses were almost ready, from postillions who were sitting very much at their ease, with long pipes in their mouths, and pots of beer on the table before them, we determined to stay no longer. This you will not be surprised at, when I tell you that the little room, in which were a dozen people smoking, was almost as hot as an oven, and probably had not been allowed to receive the fresh air for the last month. We therefore resolved to walk on before, and let the carriage follow when the postillions had finished their pipes and beer; so taking our pistols, and locking the doors of the chaise, we sallied forth to enjoy the pure air, which, cold as it was, we thought far preferable to the poisonous atmosphere of the room we had left. The night was light, and the road direct: we walked on very fast, till we got into a wood where four roads met. We knew not which to take; it was much too cold to wait there for the arrival of the carriage, and we were neither of us inclined to turn back. We therefore determined to take the broadest way, but after following it for about ten minutes, found that it terminated in three narrow paths. As I have already said, we were neither of us of a disposition to recede; so on we went, taking however that path which seemed most likely to lead towards a broader road. It was growing very dark, and so cold, that though we were well wrapped up, we almost wished ourselves in the little post-house again. In some places the shade of the trees was so thick, that we could not see our way, which obliged us to walk slowly; and I own to you I had some fears of our meeting with wild boars, the only danger we had any idea of in that country.

At length, in one place, where it was so dark that I was obliged to feel my way with my hands, to my utter astonishment I felt one of them caught by another hand, and at the same moment a hollow voice spoke some words in German, which I did not understand: I answered in French, and the person who held my hand enquired fiercely in that language; Who I was, what purpose had brought me to the wood, and why I wandered there at that late hour? By this time my master came up, and speaking the language more fluently than I did, addressed himself to the stranger; who on hearing his account, offered to lead us by a shorter way into the right road: "But," said he, "you had better first rest and warm yourselves in my habitation, which is very near, and where no pipe is ever smoked." My master immediately agreed to this proposal, which I was very glad of, for I wanted to see the end of this strange adventure. It was too dark to distinguish the person who conducted us, but we followed him by his voice, through a path so narrow, that we passed on with difficulty.

In a few minutes however, we arrived at a little plain; "And now," said he, "as we are so far from the road, I will light my lamp, and we shall pro-ceed faster." He then set fire to a few dry sticks by means of a flint, and as he was arranging the light in his lanthorn, I had an opportunity of observing his singular appearance. He wore a strange dress, somewhat resembling that of a monk, but different from any order I had ever seen: a long black robe cov-ered him from head to foot, and was tied round the waist with a cord; on his head was a large fur-cap, by his side a sabre, and in his bosom I perceived a pistol. His countenance was as uncommon as his dress; and I was sufficiently alarmed when I saw the person we were following with such confidence in that lonesome place, to induce me to take one of the pistols out of my pocket, and (taking care to speak in French) request my master to carry it for me, as I found the weight of so many inconvenient. "O!" said our companion, "you had no occasion for arms; there are seldom any intruders in this forest, and if there were, look here!" pointing to his sabre, the pistol in his breast, and a dagger which he drew from under his robe. He then quickened his pace: we followed, full of curiosity, and soon reached a little ordinary looking hut, the door of which he unlocked.

The inside had the usual appearance of a hermit's abode: a little couch, covered with a mat, at one side; an altar with a small image of the Virgin, and a lamp burning before it, on the other; a chair, a table, and a few shelves,—composed the furniture. I was sorry to see no appearance of fire, and to find the stranger's habitation very cold; but in a moment he unlocked a door opposite to that by which we had entered, and we found ourselves in a comfortable, large room, which felt quite warm. It was, like its owner, quite different from any thing I had ever seen before. The walls were covered with hangings of a sort of thick cloth, and the tiled floor with no less than three carpets one over the other. From the arched roof hung a lamp, with a number of branches, which were soon lighted, and made the room appear quite chearful. A large fire-place, with wood ready laid, immediately supplied us with a comfortable blaze, which was doubly agreeable, as we had not seen such a thing since we had been in Germany. I observed ventilators in different parts of the white-washed ceiling, and almost wondered how the place could be so warm. In this strange abode, which proved to be a sort of cave,* I remarked books, globes, musical instruments, and in short every thing that I had been accustomed to see in more civilized situations; but the most conspicuous object was a table covered with heaps of written papers.

After our conductor had made us sit down by his cheerful fire-side, and offered us refreshments which we declined, he inquired, where we were going, and whether we intended returning that way, saying how glad he should be to see us again, since fate had brought us acquainted; but intreated most earnestly that we would not direct any one to his hermitage, "for though," said he, "I have by a strange accident met with you, and I do not regret it, yet I hate mankind!" and he spoke the last words with a strong emphasis, his countenance growing more gloomy as he uttered them. For a few minutes he was silent; at length my master asked of what order he was, to which he replied with a fierce, wild look, "The order of despair." I shuddered; and he observing me, said, "Be under no uneasiness, young man. You are not in the company of a wretch loaded with crimes; my faults have been merely faults of omission, but, oh! they have led to such consequences …. I am in truth the victim of dilatoriness. I always deferred till to-morrow what ought to be done to-day.* The cruel effects of my unfortunate disposition gave too violent a blow to my mind. I have known the horrors of insanity,

and felt the hardships inflicted on such a state. I was two years in confinement. As soon as I found myself at liberty, I left the scene of my misfortunes,
and sought a country I had never seen before. Some circumstances, not
worth mentioning, induced me to fix on this cave for my abode. Here I live
unmolested. I have a friend in the town where you are going, who supplies
me with what I want. My fits of melancholy offend nobody, and however I
may be at times a burthen to myself, I am not so to any one else. I have
books and writing implements in abundance; I often sooth my disturbed
spirit with music, and I wander about this forest (which fortunately is supposed by the country people to be haunted), at all hours in freedom."

He then rose up, and telling us we had not seen all his dwelling, opened
another door, into a small bed-room, fitted up in as strange and comfortable a
style as the other; he told us, that the arrangement of this singular dwelling had
diverted his melancholy, and that he had become attached to it, from its being
his own creation, and different from every other he had seen. My master
enquired if he was a native of France (all the conversation having passed in
French); "a Frenchman the prey of despair!" said he, "no, no; I was born of
English parents in Italy." He then went to the table, and, taking up a
manuscript, added, "and I am now employed in writing an account of my life,
as a warning to persons of my disposition. If you should return here when it is
finished you shall take it away with you, but if not, leave your address, that it
may be sent to you, for to you I commit the duty of publishing, what may be a
benefit to those persons, who are inclined to put off every thing till to-
morrow."—My master was charmed at the offer, and wrote down his address
immediately. We then thought it time to depart, and our new acquaintance led
us by a short way into the road, just as our postillion, who was slowly
approaching, began to amuse himself with blowing his horn. Our extraordinary
guide retired without waiting for our thanks; and we pursued our way, talking
over our strange adventure, and resolving never to be dilatory. I am sure you
will be anxious to know whether my master ever received the promised history,
which he did in about six months after, and a very melancholy one it was.

Here Daniel paused, and I ventured to ask, whether he would not, some
time or other, tell us the story of this extraordinary man. "That I will, my
boy," said he, "though I am sure you are not one of those who want such a
lesson;" and he looked at one of my school-fellows who was older than me,
and who blushed extremely. We saw plainly from this, and many other circumstances, that our old friend was acquainted with every thing that concerned us, and we were at no loss to discover how he procured his
information, as we knew that our school-master frequently took a glass of ale
at the cottage of an evening, after we had all gone home.

CHAPTER XI.

THE PASSING OF THE PYRENEAN MOUNTAINS.

THE next Wednesday was a half-holiday,* and the weather being favourable, we assembled at old Daniel's door, but were delayed to rather a later hour than usual, by an accident which happened on the way. One of the little boys, who was very impatient to arrive before the rest, that he might have Trusty all to himself for a few minutes, would cross a ditch (though repeatedly warned of what must be the consequence) by way of a short cut, and fell in; but as he was a good-natured fellow, we were all ready to assist him; so we helped him to scrape the mud off his stockings and trowsers, and then pursued our way. Daniel, on seeing him in this condition, immediately enquired the cause of his disaster, and on being told that it was because he would not take the advice of those who knew the place better than he did, blamed him extremely, and said, I will tell you what a danger-ous situation I once brought myself into, by acting just as you have done. Then, having distributed the apples as usual, he spoke as follows.

ABOUT fifty-five years ago I spent some time at a little town in the south of France, at the foot of the Pyrenees, which you know are the high mountains that separate France from Spain, and here I became acquainted with some very agreeable young men, who were natives of that place. As I could speak the language tolerably, I enjoyed the pleasure of their society very much, and joined in all their dancing and gaiety. I think they were the merriest people I ever knew; and I should have been quite happy among them, but that my dear master had not perfectly recovered his strength after a tedious ague, which had attacked him the autumn before, and which prevented his exploring the mountains as he had intended.

One of the young men in whose acquaintance I found so much satisfac-tion, had a brother, who, in consequence of being accused of having killed a man in a duel (a sad custom then too common in that country),* had been obliged to abscond, and remained concealed, until the affair (in which he had not been to blame) could be cleared up. He had only crossed a moun-tain, into the Spanish territory, where he was perfectly safe, and used fre-quently to steal back to his family, especially on occasion of any festivity. He was generally accompanied to the French side by some of his Spanish friends, and some of his countrymen used to escort them back under pretence of botanizing,* or searching for minerals among the mountains; so that, notwithstanding the risks he ran in these excursions, they afforded much pleasure to him and his young companions.

I had been some months in that country before I met the young man who had absconded, but I had become very intimate with his brother, who was one of my greatest favourites, and was acquainted with all the secrets of the family. At length the day of his feast approached (that is, the saint's day whose name he bore),* and on the eve at midnight he arrived, with three young Spaniards who came to join in the festivities. It was a most joyful meeting; all his sisters had little presents prepared for him, and all his friends, who were intrusted with the secret of his being at home, brought him boxes of comfits, or some trifle of that sort to show their good-will, according to the custom of the country. He remained three days, during which there was continual feasting and gaiety; and I really believe the pleasure of the dancing, music, and festivity, was heightened by the slight mixture of danger that attended his visit. When all this was over, and the hour of his departure approached, a party determined to accompany him half-way over the mountain, and I insisted on being one of them. My master remonstrated and advised that I should not attempt it, as he knew I was not a good mountain-walker, and was besides out of practice just at that time. Several of the natives of the place mentioned, that we should have a large tract of ground to pass over, where there was no habitation, and which was lately become dangerous on account of the snow, which drove the wild beasts from the higher mountains: they represented that what might be an easy matter to persons accustomed to such expeditions, would be very perilous for me, and recommended strenuously that I should relinquish my design; but I was, like my young friend here, resolved to go my own way.

We set off about six o'clock in the evening, the weather very fine, but very cold: our party consisted of the young man and his three Spanish friends, his brother, another Frenchman and myself. Those who were to cross the mountain entirely were well armed, but we who intended to go but half-way, carried only long poles, besides our baskets, with the things necessary to give an appearance of botanizing to our excursion in case of meeting with any of the patroles,* which at that time, on some political account (I forget what), were stationed on many parts of the mountains. It was not considered safe for the fugitive to risk being recognized by any of these, and therefore we took a round to avoid them.

We had not proceeded very far up the hill, when I, who was not habituated to this sort of exercise, began to grow tired, and my companions were obliged to slacken their pace on that account; and at length I became so weak, and they so cold, that we knew not what to do. Just at that moment we perceived the glistening of arms at a distance, and finding that it was impossible to avoid meeting the patrole, we resolved to go boldly forward to the guard-house, and ask permission to warm and rest ourselves. One of our party, who had more presence of mind than the rest, advanced first, and representing to the soldiers that we were poor fellows who had been botanizing, and had lost our way, obtained permission for us to sit down a few minutes by their fire, which was indeed a most cheerful spectacle at such a time. However, we had scarcely begun to feel the warmth of the blaze, when we were chilled with terror, by one of the soldiers enquiring if we had met any travellers in our way; for that they had received intelligence, that the young man who had killed the Chevalier de B. was certainly to come from the Spanish side about that time, and that the Chevalier's relations had promised a handsome reward, to the man who should seize his murderer. One of them then handed a written description of the young man to his brother, who pretended to read it attentively, for the purpose of placing himself between the lamp and the subject of the paper; I took out my herbal,* and pointed out some particular herbs to the soldier next me, telling him how difficult I had found it to procure them, and what dangers I had run in the search, whilst one of the Spaniards attracted the attention of the rest, by taking a bottle of strong wine out of his pocket, and dividing it with them. His example was soon followed by others of the party, and the soldiers never thought of examining our poor friend, who sat wrapped in his cloak close to the fire, and appeared colder than any of us. After resting there about a quarter of an hour, we took leave of the soldiers, one of whom called after us to say, that he hoped if we met such a person as we read the description of, we would find some means to send him to their guard-house. The young man himself answered, "Oh, yes, you may depend on us;" and we pursued our way, very glad to have escaped this danger so well. We then continued slowly ascending the mountain, till we reached an extensive plain where I was able to walk as fast as the rest, so that we soon arrived at the extremity of it, and here we parted with the Spaniards and their French companion. We then endeavoured to make our way back as quick as possible, but unfortunately, before we had got half-way, a violent shower of snow came on, which entirely concealed all surrounding objects from our view, and prevented our being able to distinguish our road. In this dilemma, we resolved to seek the shelter of a shepherd's hut which we had observed in our way, and to remain there until the shower was over. You perceive, my young friends, that all these difficulties occurred, in consequence of my undertaking this expedition contrary to the advice of persons who knew better than me; for had I not occasioned so many delays, my friends would have probably reached the guard-house before the snow-shower came on.

After great search and difficulty, we at length discovered the hut, which remained useless in winter, and only served as a shelter from the heat of the summer's sun to the shepherds who drove their flocks up to this fine pasture at that season of the year. It was very small, and being built of sticks and straw, we should have found it tolerably warm, had there been a door to close against the inclemency of the weather; but this we were not so fortunate to discover: however we were very glad to perceive a heap of straw in one corner, and as there was no appearance of the snow abating, and as my two companions were also fatigued by this time, they readily agreed to my plan of resting till the dawn. It was now twelve o'clock, and we had been walking since six, so that we were very well pleased to lie down; and spreading out our straw in the warmest part of the hut, we stretched ourselves on it, lying close together like pigs. My two companions were soon asleep, but cold and fatigue kept me awake, and I sincerely wished I had followed the good advice which would have placed me in my warm bed at that hour. At length I began to doze, when I was startled by a very loud snore (as I thought) at the other side of the hut; I listened and heard it repeated again and again. I then heard heavy footsteps pass the door, and go round our habitation two or three times. I knew not what to think of this, but considered that it would be better to awaken my companions, which I did with some difficulty, and as soon as I had described to them what I had heard, one of them jumped up and ran to the door, while the other again fell asleep. In a few minutes the young man who had gone out, returned in great terror, to inform us that there were two monstrous bears* walking about our hut, and that as we had no weapons of defence but our sticks, we could not possibly escape, if once they found their way in. He therefore roused his lazy companion, and after we had placed our sticks across the door-way, so as to form some obstacle to the entrance, we again lay down on our straw, where he who had neither heard the sounds that terrified me, nor seen the objects that had alarmed the other, after laughing at what he called our ridiculous fears, went to sleep again in a few minutes. He who had beheld the bears, had as little rest I imagine as myself, and at the first dawn we awoke our tranquil companion, and sallied forth to pursue our way; and you may imagine how we must have been shocked, at perceiving the snow all round the place of our shelter marked with the prints of our shaggy visitors' feet, and that the mere accident of the beasts' unwieldiness, had saved us from being torn to pieces. We reached the end of our journey without any more adventures, and you may be assured I took care ever after, especially in strange places, to follow the advice of those who were better informed than myself.

We were greatly delighted with the story of the bears, which was something new to us, and asked our old friend a number of questions about those ugly animals that were so near devouring him. We also enquired about the construction of the hut, and agreed that it would be very amusing to build such in the summer-holidays, in which the good Daniel promised to assist us. I must not forget to tell you, that I dreamt of the bears that night, and thought I fought most valiantly with one of them.

CHAPTER XII.

DOG TRUSTY'S ANCESTOR.

THE next Sunday we found old Daniel in remarkable high spirits, with a new coat and a new hat; old Susan also in a new gown, with a pink ribbon in her cap, and as to the entertainment I had never seen it so splendid. There were cakes, gingerbread-nuts, apples, pears, and plums, and we had all a larger share than usual. The old man asked if any of us were born on that day, and seemed disappointed to find us all answer in the negative; "for," said he, "my young friends, you must know, this is my birth-day. Exactly ninety-four years ago, I came into the world, and that is the reason you see Susan and me so handsomely dressed to-day. We always make merry with our friends on this occasion, and though the poor child cannot hear what is said, she sees that we look happy, and that satisfies her:" and he said the truth, for Susan looked delighted, when she saw how pleased we were with the nice treat she had prepared for us. Old Daniel then, patting Trusty's head, and giving him a cake, said, The story I am now going to tell you, concerns one of Trusty's ancestors, and is an adventure that I had on this day fifty-nine years ago.

During my travels with the same good friend I have so often mentioned to you, we spent some time at Naples, a land of wonders with which I was charmed. Among the many curiosities we went to see, was the *Grotto del Cane* (or dog's grotto), so called because the effect of a poisonous vapour which rises in it to a certain height, is generally exhibited on one of that species. The day we went to see it, a poor animal was brought with a cord about his neck, who followed very contentedly till we came near the grotto; he then began to struggle and moan; but when at last the door was opened, giving a most piteous cry, he sprung from the man who held him, and ran to my master: then lying down at his feet, looked up at him in such a beseeching manner, and so plainly intreated his protection, that he instantly made a friend of the generous-hearted man, who declared he would rather submit to have the experiment tried on himself, than subject the animal to it that had thrown itself on his mercy. He then gave some money to the owner of the dog, who was very glad to get rid of him, for he said, he did not imagine he could have supported the experiment more than once again, as he had already suffered by it. This accounted for the dog's terror when he approached the grotto; but the singularity of his selecting my master for his champion always appeared very extraordinary.

We returned to Naples in triumph with our new acquisition. He was an ugly, half-starved animal, but said, "I thank you," so plain in every look and movement, that it was impossible for my master not to be attached to him, and I loved him for his sake. Often he has said to me, "Well, Dan, of all the compliments ever paid me on my looks" (and you must know he was a remarkably handsome man), "none has ever flattered me so much as that of poor Chance." We fed and took excellent care of our poor dog, and in a short time he was another thing: not so handsome as Trusty, but a very sleek, smooth, good-looking fellow. He assumed the privilege of sleeping in his master's room, and always placed himself somewhere near the door, as if he was determined to guard it against all intruders. By the time we left Naples, we had become so fond of Chance, that we allowed him a place in the carriage without regret.

It was about two months after, that we were travelling in a wild part of the country, after heavy rains which had made the roads so bad that they were almost impassable. In several places the carriage was prevented from oversetting merely by the assistance of men, who supported it with ropes, sometimes on one side and sometimes on the other. One evening about four o'clock, our postillion stopped suddenly at the gate of a large, deserted-looking house, where he said we must remain till morning. My master remonstrated, and represented to him, that it was a very early hour to stop for the night, but he declared he could not answer for the consequences if we were to go on, as the road was even worse than what we had already passed; besides, if we did not stop here, as there was no other house within many miles of this, we must travel a long time in the night, which would be very dark, and might subject us to dangers of more than one sort. We enquired if he had ever been in this house before, hoping that at any rate he was acquainted with the place he had brought us to; but he said, "No; though he had often passed by it." Finding there was no remedy, we were at length persuaded to enter the building, which was a most desolate-looking abode, where there was scarcely a whole window to be seen. It appeared to have been erected for a barrack, or something of that sort, but we saw no inhabitants except three men, a father and his two sons, whose countenances had a mixed expression of ferocity and sullenness, which gave us no reason to hope for a hospitable reception. They came slowly to the gate, one by one, and on our asking if the house were an inn, replied in the affirmative, but shewed none of that alacrity which one expects to meet with at such places. With some difficulty the great gate was opened to admit the carriage, and here the building shewed, if possible, a more dreary appearance, than at the outside. The grass was grown over the pavement, and there did not seem to be a window unbroken: some of these were stuffed with straw, but the greater number admitted the cold air, which whistled through the long galleries of the extensive fabrick.

The inn-keeper and his sons appeared quite unaccustomed to receive travellers, and when we enquired for a room, told us we might go up stairs and chuse amongst them, for they were all unoccupied, but did not offer to conduct us. We ascended the broken stair-case, and explored a number of apartments, all equally uninhabitable; but at length we discovered one very large, containing three beds, and in which only one out of three windows was broke. Here we resolved to rest; and after several vain efforts, at last persuaded one of the men to bring us some wood and make a fire, which was perfectly necessary, as the evening was extremely cold, and the house felt like a vault. It was equally difficult to procure any food; and I thought myself very lucky, when I procured for my master a soup made of vermicelli, salt, and water, and some fried liver. I then went to enquire about other necessary matters, and was surprised to find, that in a place professing to be an inn, they could only supply us with three sheets. I enquired the cause of this scarcity, and was told that, about a week before, a banditti which infested that part of the country, had come and carried off every thing the house contained, a thing by no means uncommon in that lonesome situation. I then asked some other questions of the man who had given this account, who answered very sullenly with a down look, until I had the imprudence to say I wondered how he could have the hardiness to stay in such a place; when he gave a sort of involuntary side-glance so ferocious, that I immediately formed conjectures, very unfavourable to him, and disagreeable to myself at such a moment. He answered however carelessly, that poor people must earn their bread where they could; and then carried wood up stairs to replenish the fire. As soon as we were alone, I communicated my observations and suspicions to my master, and we agreed that it would be necessary to be on our guard, especially as we were not perfectly sure of our postillion's honesty or good intentions in bringing us to this house. My master then imparted to me some remarks he had made during my absence. He had amused himself with reading the scribbling on different parts of the walls,* and pointed out to me two instances, that appeared then of an alarming nature, though we should have laughed at them, had we been otherwise circumstanced. They were written in Italian, and so badly spelt, that it was with difficulty we could make them out: the translation of one was, "Take care of yourselves, you are in a dangerous place!" and that of the other, "Travellers, beware, beware of the master of this house!" You may imagine how disagreeable all this was, when we had no remedy. Our room was so perfectly bare of furniture, that we could not have any apprehension of people being concealed in it; there was but one door, and the windows were at a great distance from the ground; we therefore flattered ourselves, that by locking our door, and leaving our loaded pistols on the table, we should be tolerably secure against any surprize, and we agreed that we would not yield without a desperate struggle.

We had been much fatigued with a very disagreeable day's journey, of which we had walked a great deal, and therefore went to bed very early; our poor dog, who was also very much tired, taking possession of a vacant bed next the door. For some time after we lay down, I listened and started up every time the wood crackled in the chimney; but at length we all fell into a sound sleep. How long this had lasted I know not, when I was awaked by a little noise, and to my utter horror and astonishment, distinguished by the glimmering light which the fire still gave, a tall man, with a dagger in his hand, stealing gently across the room towards my master's bed, and immediately after another, who seemed to be directing his steps towards mine. I had been so sure that any attempt to open the door (which I had carefully locked) would have put us on our guard, that I had not taken the precaution of placing the pistols within my reach, and just as I was considering whether it would be possible by suddenly darting across the room, to seize them, Chance started out of his sleep, flew at the man who was approaching my master, and bit his leg. I then ran to the pistols, and the second person immediately made his escape. In the mean time my master had collared the man whom the dog had attacked; but the villain stabbed him in the hand, and then by a dexterous twist gained the door, and ran down the gallery to the stairs, where I did not think it prudent to pursue him. In fact, the whole transaction passed so rapidly, that it was almost like a dream.

As soon as I had assisted my master to tie a handkerchief on his wounded hand, I again went to fasten the door, which I was much surprised to find had been opened; but after having locked it, on trying whether it was fast, I found that the lock was useless, and we as much exposed as before. We then resolved to place against the door a heavy bench and clumsy table which were in the room, and having thus secured ourselves against surprize, we returned to our beds, and slept quietly till morning, when we discovered that the villains had not come to no purpose, for a small box, of which I had unfortunately appeared particularly careful, was missing; and as it contained, amongst other things of less importance, a miniature picture of great value to my master, I was very much vexed.

The moment I perceived it was day-light, I went down-stairs to waken our postillion, for we were most anxious to depart; and in the passage, I met one of our landlords, who hoped we had rested well. I mentioned to him the nocturnal adventure, at which he at first expressed great astonishment, but then said it was not impossible that some thieves should have got into the house, as it was so ill secured. He begged to know if we had lost any thing, and on my saying that a box had been taken, which contained nothing of value except a miniature picture, I thought he looked very much disappointed. I afterwards met the others, who spoke nearly in the same manner; but I fancied one of them looked more confused than the rest.

Anxious to get out of this dismal place, I hurried the postillion, whose countenance shewed no symptoms of guilt, and who really expressed surprise and terror when he heard what had passed; and as soon as the carriage was ready, my master, with the faithful Chance at his heels, descended the stairs, at the foot of which the three men stood; but the moment the dog saw them, he flew at one of the sons,* and caught him by the leg, nor could any thing induce him to relinquish his hold, until my master knelt down by him, and put his fingers in his mouth to extricate the unfortunate man. This accident betrayed the whole affair; an immediate confession was extorted from the wretches, who promised to return the box on condition my master would not accuse them to the magistrates: he was satisfied on having the picture of his dear friend restored, and we continued our journey, better pleased than ever with having behaved humanely to poor Chance. He lived to be very old, and had frequent opportunities of shewing his gratitude in the course of his life. While my master lived, he was never without one of his breed, and since his death, I have always kept one of them with me.

We were delighted with this story of Trusty's ancestor, and bestowed a double portion of caresses on his descendant this evening. We talked the matter over as usual, when we ran to our oak-tree, and thought, what a fortunate thing it was for the poor dog to have met with such a good master. We concluded by resolving always to treat brutes with the greatest humanity, in imitation of this worthy man who was so well rewarded for his.

CHAPTER XIII.

THE BOY WHO WAS FORGOT AT SCHOOL.

THERE was a little boy among us that had come to the school just before me, whom everybody liked very much. He was very attentive to his book, learned with facility, and was extremely good-natured; but in consequence of having been treated very harshly before he was placed at our school, he had got a sad cowardly trick of telling falsehoods upon all occasions. He was always ready to deny the most trifling circumstance that occurred, and all the kindness and gentleness of our master was insufficient to correct him. At length the matter was communicated to old Daniel, as we discovered on Sunday, when he said, I am sorry to find that after all the stories I have told on the subject of telling lies, there should still be any of my little friends infected with such a mean, cowardly vice. I hope no one of this description may ever think of being a soldier, for I should expect to hear of his running away from the enemy, if he had not courage even to speak truth.

This has brought to my mind, continued Daniel (after a short pause during which old Susan distributed the fruit), a story which made a great impression on me, and which may possibly entertain you as well as any other I could recollect at this moment. I was once sent with my regiment to assist the troops of a foreign land, where a dangerous insurrection had taken place. The inhabitants of a large tract of country had become disaffected to their lawful rulers, and the consequences were horrible in the extreme. I was so unfortunate as to be a witness on that occasion of all the dreadful accidents of civil war, and I would rather see a year of hard service in any other way, than one month of such transactions as usually take place in similar situations. We found the country-people irritated by the ill conduct of their own military, who I am sorry to say frequently behaved more like gangs of plundering banditti, than parties of regular troops, and the soldiers continually harrassed by the peasantry, who thought they beheld in every military habit a tyrant. However I must say there were some places where the people were not oppressed, and here the native soldiers were rather considered as protectors.

Immediately on our landing we were sent to a little town, where we were placed under the command of an officer who was a native of that country, and had been appointed governor of a certain small district, which he continued to keep in perfect submission, by a prudent mixture of mildness and severity, and by inforcing the strictest discipline amongst the troops. The town in which we were quartered was extremely pleasant, the inhabitants peaceable, though by no means well affected towards their rulers, and the habits of life more cheerful than could have been expected at such a time; but they were accustomed to hear continually of wars, and their amusements were not to be interrupted till the enemy was literally at their gates. The governor's wife and children, and also the families of many of his officers, lodged in the town, and with the addition of those of some of the town's-people, formed a very agreeable society, which my master constantly frequented. The governor's house was situated at one extremity of the town, and as I had often occasion to go there about my master's business, I used sometimes to see his little boys. There were five of them, but only four lived at home; the eldest, who was nine years old, had lately been placed at a very good school which happened to be in the town, and I never saw him at his father's house but of a Sunday.

We had remained in perfect tranquillity about two months, and by the accounts daily received from other places, had every reason to hope that all would be brought to a conclusion very soon, without our little chearful abode being disturbed by the approach of danger, when suddenly, one morning between three and four o'clock, the drum beat to arms, and the whole town was thrown into confusion. Everyone was alarmed, but no one well knew why. The soldiers were running to the square which was always the place of rendezvous, the women were asking news in the streets, and the young children were crying, because they saw those about them in consternation. I must confess that I had been thrown off my guard by too much security, and was more confused by this sudden call than I ought to have been; however I instantly hastened to my master, whom I met at the door of his apartment prepared for fight, and as we issued forth, we learnt from passing troops, that a large party was advancing with all speed against the town, that they had already approached very near, and that their numbers were so superior to ours, that we could not hope to come off conquerors. It was determined to send the women and children with the baggage, to a town about twenty miles off which had fortifications, and a strong garrison, and all we could expect was to impede the progress of the enemy until these were lodged in a place of safety. Meanwhile fresh accounts arrived every moment of the near approach of the hostile troops, and we all marched out to meet them, with a determination to make their conquest as difficult we could. We met them just outside the town, on a little plain, where we had a most desperate battle, which however lasted but a short time. I got this wound in my right hand, and also one in my left leg on that occasion, but the pain I felt at being obliged to retreat was more severe than that of my wounds. In fact I must confess (and I should not be ashamed of it) we fled into the town in great confusion, and had just time to close the gates against our pursuers, and thus gain an interval to make our retreat sure. We had the satisfaction of hearing that the women and children had made their escape, and were happy to be able to effect ours to a rising ground flanked by a wood, about a mile on the other side of the town. Here the enemy ceased to molest us, their object appearing to be to gain possession of the town, and in a few hours we continued our retreat to the place where our fugitives had already taken refuge. I will not attempt to give you an account of our meeting, or an idea of the lamentations of those who had lost their friends, and of those who had to attend on persons they loved, wounded almost to death. These are horrible sights, and though I am a soldier every inch of me, I can never think coolly of the four-and-twenty hours that follow after a battle. Our commanding officer was but slightly hurt; my own wounds were not severe; and my dear master had (almost miraculously) escaped uninjured.

We supposed nothing was missing, except one baggage-cart of comparatively small value, and two of the soldiers' wives who were no great loss, until the governor on entering the house where his family were lodged, immediately enquired for his eldest son, who was his favourite child, and a most promising boy. His wretched mother, who was in agonies of grief, was scarcely able to inform him, that in the confusion of the morning, the child, who was at school on the other side of the town, had been forgotten: she had still endeavoured to flatter* herself on the way, that he would be found amongst the straggling groups that followed at various distances, but on their arrival had ascertained that no one had seen or even thought of him. She then burst into a flood of tears, and with all the absurdity of a very weak woman as she was, declared she was sure he had been murdered. This idea her husband combated with every possible argument, yet (poor man!) his terrors, though more rational, were scarcely inferior to her own. He thought of the forlorn situation of a child of nine years old, without money or friends, for he supposed the school-master would have his own affairs to attend to in such a critical moment; and in the present circumstances he saw no possibility of speedily recovering the poor boy. In fact the governor's situation was more to be pitied than that of many of those who were desperately wounded, and every one partook of his distress, for he was a worthy man, and made no whining complaints. I have always felt most interested for those who endured most silently.

Next morning, at an early hour, we were much surprised by hearing that a flag of truce appeared at a distance, and in a few minutes after that a baggage cart with two women and a child were among the soldiers who brought it. You may suppose we immediately guessed who they were, and that all the formalities of receiving them were gone through as rapidly as possible. Their sole business was to escort the boy, and deliver him into the hands of his father (for I suppose the cart and the two women were thrown into the bargain as good-for-nothing lumber), and with him they brought a letter from the conquering chief, signifying to the governor, that the writer was happy to have an opportunity of rendering a service to a man, who had behaved with so much humanity to his poor countrymen.

As soon as the first violence of joy and congratulations were over, the child was questioned relative to what had passed. He said, that on the first alarm most of the boys had run away to their different homes, and the master had hastened to another part of the town, to protect some valuable property that he possessed there: he himself did not wake till some people rushed into the room where he slept, to take away their children who also inhabited the same apartment: he then got up and dressed himself, not well knowing the cause of all this bustle and noise; but on going to different parts of the house he found it quite deserted, not a human being remaining in it, but an old deaf man who knew as little about what was passing as himself. On going into the street, he learned that his mother and all her family had escaped from the town many hours before, and that his father and the troops under his command had been beaten, and retreated a short time before, and in fact that the enemy were then about to march in. Just at that moment he met one of the two soldiers' wives who had been left behind, who desired him to stay by her, and to be sure, if he was asked whose child he was, for his life not to tell, but to say he was the son of one of the serjeants.* This he had refused positively to do; for he had so often heard his father and mother say that people ought never to tell a lie on any occasion, and that God took care of those who spoke the truth, that he was determined to answer truly to any questions that should be put to him. To the first officer who asked who that little boy was, the woman answered before he could speak, that he was the son of one of the serjeants who had fled, and the officer passed on. To a second she gave a similar answer; but at length a third putting the question to the child himself, he replied boldly, that he was the governor's son, who had been forgotten when the rest of his family escaped. This man immediately took him with him to a place where a number of the enemy's officers were assembled. Here he was asked a variety of questions, tending to ascertain whether he really was the person he pretended to be, and had the pleasure of hearing the greatest commendations of his father's justice and mild conduct, all the officers agreeing that his son ought to be sent to him in safety without delay. He was fed and taken care of that day, by the two women, who were allowed to accompany him; and next morning they were all sent off in the manner I have mentioned. This affair made a great impression on my mind, as it proved the advantages of mildness in command, of strict attention to military discipline, and of courageous adherence to truth. The rest of this campaign was full of horrors; but tranquillity was at length restored to that unfortunate country; and I am happy to be able to tell you, that the worthy governor and his family were restored to their home before we embarked for our native land.

We were all much pleased with this story, and the little boy for whom it was particularly intended, seemed to be extremely interested. Indeed a proof of the effect produced on him by the relation of it appeared the next day. A little flower-pot, that stood in a window of the passage going to our school-room, had been broken, and no one knew how the accident had happened; our master appeared inclined to suspect one of the boys who had frequently done aukward things; but just as he began to speak on the subject, Charles stept forward, and in a very pompous manner avowed his having thrown down the flower-pot, and also that he was able and willing to replace it with another. This offer the master did not think proper to accept, but he highly commended the boy who had courage to own what he had done: indeed he made a display of approbation on this occasion, that he would not have done had the circumstance occurred to any one else, and some of us very well understood this. Some children have a great deal of penetration and we had very observing lads among us.

CHAPTER XIV.

THE MAN-HATER RESUMED.

WE now began to fear that every new story would be the last. It was past the middle of October, but the weather was remarkably mild for the time of year, and Daniel had not yet talked of desisting from his stories. However they became every day more precious, and we listened with more attention (if possible) than at first, which seemed to give great pleasure to our old friend.

Some private affairs of our school-master about this time occasioned him to give us several half-holidays, and we took care to profit by them in assembling round the good Daniel's porch. At last he said, "I believe, my boys, you think I am made of stories; but I must soon leave off, for the weather begins to grow cold and uncertain." We all looked at each other with quite doleful countenances, which made the old man smile, and he added, "but I hope we may have two or three more fine days before we finish for this year." I then ventured to remind him of the story of the strange man he met in the forest, which we were all longing to hear. "You have given me a difficult task, my young friend (said he), for it is more than half a century since I saw the manuscript, and I never read it but twice, once when it first came into my master's possession, and once about five years after. However, as I have often related some of the principal incidents, I hope I shall be able to gratify your curiosity, which I allow is extremely natural. It was a large manuscript, which my poor master valued highly; who got it after his death I never could learn. What I can remember you shall hear.

THIS gentleman, whom I shall call by his christian name Henry, was the son of an English merchant, who had been many years settled at Leghorn,* in the full enjoyment of all the wealth and luxury that prosperous trade can bestow. The success of his commercial speculations was unbounded, and the splendour in which he lived, as described in the manuscript, appeared almost fabulous. He had three children, two sons and a daughter; Louisa was the eldest, Henry a year younger, and Felix seven years the junior of his brother. These children were all idolized by their parents, and brought up with a degree of extravagant indulgence, which does not agree with every disposition. Their wishes were prevented* on all occasions, their faults winked at, and their caprices continually gratified. Henry, naturally of an indolent temper, was much injured by this sort of education; he acquired habits of procrastination which appeared almost like a disease, and was scarcely capable of making the commonest exertions. This fault excepted, his character appeared to be very amiable; he was candid, brave, and good-natured, but his good-nature seldom produced any corresponding effects, as he always deferred till too late those kind actions which his heart prompted him to perform. I cannot relate to you a tenth part of the instances of this unfortunate disposition described in the manuscript (and these the writer said were but a small part of what he might have mentioned), but I will tell you some few that I recollect.

Henry had a dog that he was extremely fond of (such a good honest fellow as Trusty I suppose), who used to sleep at his door every night, and accompany him when he went out walking or boating. It happened one day that a party being made to spend a few days at a villa some miles distant from Leghorn, Henry, who was always last, was so hurried to join the company, that he locked the door on his dog, and never recollected till he had gone half-way, that the poor animal was shut up in an inner room of his apartment, from whence no one could release him till he sent back the key. He thought of sending a servant with it immediately, but (according to his usual custom) deferred it till he should reach the villa, and when he arrived there, totally forgot his intention. At night he again recollected it, but again put it off, resolving to send the key early next morning. In this way three days passed, and as he was returning on the fourth to Leghorn, he felt very uneasy. As he ascended the stairs that led to his apartment, he listened for the barking of his dog, but heard no noise: he then asked a servant whom he met, whether they had heard the animal since his departure: the woman answered, "O yes, for the first two days he made a great noise, and we tried to let him out; but since yesterday morning we have not heard him." Henry proceeded in silence to the door of his chamber; he trembled as he unlocked the closet: the first object he beheld was his dog lying dead. He lifted him up, but he was stiff and cold. This sad circumstance affected him for a few days, and he determined not to act in the same manner any more; but similar things continually occurred, many of which were detailed in the manuscript.

One more circumstance I particularly recollect, that happened when he was still a child. Some beautiful foreign birds were given him, with a direction to feed them only on a particular kind of seed, which accompanied the cage. He was charmed with the present, and resolved to take the greatest care of these rare creatures, who were covered with the most beautiful plumage and sung delightfully. Every day he grew fonder of his birds, and as the seed with which he was to feed them was only to be procured at one shop, he resolved to lay in a good supply of it, before what they had should be exhausted. The seed however diminished rapidly, and he still deferred sending for more; but one morning he found the birds' cage without any food, and the poor animals, who had been many hours starving, pining for want of nourishment. He then determined to send immediately for seed, but by some accident this was delayed till evening. In the mean time the birds had nothing to eat, for the person who had brought them to Leghorn had declared that it would kill them to take any sort of food, but that which he had specified. In the evening the seed was put into the cage in great abundance; the birds looked sick, but Henry was in hopes they would be quite well in the morning: however, when he went to look at them the moment he was up, he found one already dead, and the other in the last convulsions. He was greatly distressed, and imagined they had been poisoned, but the seed on being examined proved to be perfectly good, and a person who understood those sort of things, assured him they had died in consequence of eating too much after long fasting. Henry was very sorry, and resolved not to put off any thing again; but he continued the same notwithstanding all his good intentions.

When he was about fifteen, he one evening obtained permission to take his little brother out walking, and felt very proud of being trusted to take care of him without a servant. The child was, like most other children, particularly fond of gathering shells on the sea-shore, and thither the brothers directed their steps. As soon as they had got to a retired part of the shore, Henry, who had taken a good deal of exercise in the morning, sat down to rest, while the little Felix searched among the pebbles for shells. Four or five times the child brought handfuls of them to his brother, but at length he ran to a greater distance, and Henry began to wonder at his not returning; he thought of going to seek him immediately, but as he was reading an entertaining book, he thought he might as well finish the chapter first, and that by that time Felix would probably return. Three quarters of an hour elapsed, and the child did not appear; Henry then began to be alarmed, and whilst he sought his brother among the rocks, felt very sorry that he had not gone sooner. Repeatedly he called Felix, but no answer was returned. He was seriously unhappy at this, and walked for an hour backward and forward on the shore, asking all those he saw, whether they had seen a child answering the description of his brother; but all answered in the negative, until he met an infirm old woman, who replied to his enquiries that she had indeed seen the child, and a melancholy sight it was; she then begged of him to come with her; and as he followed trembling with terror, she informed him that she had seen at a distance a little boy on a rock, amusing himself with gathering shells, who, ignorant of the place, had remained till the coming in of the tide had surrounded him with water; that she, observing his danger, had gone as near him as she could, to try if she could give assistance, which any person not absolutely weak with age and infirmity might easily have done, and that when she found it was impossible for her to be of any use, she had hastened to seek for help, but unfortunately all the neighbourhood had followed a procession, and she could meet with no one; she had heard the child's cries a long time, but supposed he must now be drowned, for the water was rising every moment, and he stood on a little point of the rock, the only part which remained dry. I shall not repeat to you the dreadful description that poor Henry gave of his feelings. The body of the little Felix was found, and his unfortunate brother was prevented from beholding the misery into which his family was plunged, by a violent fever, attended with delirium, which brought him to the brink of the grave. No one ever knew how much he was to blame for the death of his young brother, and though he remained very melancholy for some time, yet at last the elasticity of youthful spirits raised him from this sad state, and in another year he had recovered the effects of this cruel misfortune; though sometimes, when he gazed on the pale face of his mother, he could not help recollecting that she did not look so wan before the death of her little Felix."

Here Daniel stopped, and telling us that it was too long a story for him to relate at one time, promised he would continue it at our next meeting. I assure you what we had already heard made us quite grave, and the boy to whom the old man had given a hint on the subject at a former meeting, looked almost as if he had been guilty of all these faults. However, when we reached our oak-tree, we all cheered up, and in a few minutes got rid of the sorrowful impression caused by the death of Felix.

CHAPTER XV.

THE MAN-HATER CONCLUDED.

THE next holiday we were rather earlier than our usual time, and Daniel, perceiving our impatience, hastened to distribute his fruit, and began as follows.

MANY circumstances were related in the manuscript, of the next five years of the unhappy Henry's life, all tending to prove the baneful effects of this unfortunate indolence of disposition, which made his too indulgent father and mother very miserable; but as I do not well remember them, I shall pass on to one which occurred when he was about twenty, and which made a great impression on my memory.

He had a friend about his own age, to whom he was very much attached, and who loved him so well, that he was almost blind to his most glaring imperfections. One evening he received a hurried note from this young man, intreating he would come to him in the utmost haste. He wondered what Antonio, whom he had parted from but a few hours before, could want with him in such a hurry, and called for his messenger that he might enquire, but the boy who had brought the note had immediately gone away. Henry determined at any rate to go directly, but still he lay stretched at full length on his sopha* in his wrapping gown and slippers, conjecturing for what purpose his friend should desire to see him so suddenly. At length he got up and arranged his dress; but between all delays a full hour had passed before he was ready to go out: on finding so much time had elapsed, he was almost tempted to defer going till the next day, but his curiosity overcoming his indolence, he went to the house of his friend. When he arrived there, he was much surprised to find that Antonio was not at home; he enquired how long it was since he had gone out, and was told that it was about a quarter of an hour after the return of the messenger that he had sent for him: the servant added, that he had gone out soon after two gentlemen who had paid him an afternoon-visit, that he had observed him take his sword, and that they all three looked extremely angry. Before Henry could at all arrange his ideas, quite distracted by this account, a great bustle in the hall attracted his attention, and in a few minutes the bleeding body of his friend was brought in. As they placed Antonio on the sopha he fainted, but soon recovering, he looked round him, and observing Henry, turned his dying eyes on him, and said in a faint voice, "Alas! Henry, I have then been mistaken." These were the last words he spoke. The surgeons arrived to examine his wounds, and immediately pronounced them to be mortal. In half an hour he died.

Henry leaned over him to his last moment, an image of silent despair. He reproached himself for not coming instantly on receiving the note, and thought that he perhaps might have been able to prevent the dreadful catastrophe; but judge of the horror he must have felt, when, a few hours after poor Antonio had breathed his last, he received the following account of this fatal affair. The two young men, who were intimates of Antonio's family, had come in high spirits to pay him a friendly visit, and prevailed on him to join them in a masquerade-party, which they had planned for the next week. He agreed, and proposed that Henry should also be let into the secret, and invited to make one among them; this they did not approve, on account of the procrastinating temper of the young man, which would prevent his being exact to the time, and because an omission of this sort would spoil all their amusement. Antonio promised faithfully for his friend, that he should be as punctual as any of the rest, but could not persuade them to admit him of their party. This rather put him out of humour, and when they began to rally* him on his enthusiastic friendship for Henry, and one of them at length went so far as to say he was convinced Henry felt no such attachment for him, Antonio fiercely demanded what reason he had for such an opinion? The other replied as fiercely, that it was because he knew a person of his disposition was utterly incapable of being a warm friend. One word brought on another; both were violent in their tempers, and in a few minutes became so exasperated against each other, that it was determined to decide the quarrel immediately by the sword. Antonio's antagonist had his friend with him, and the note to Henry before-mentioned was written in consequence of this decision. They both sneered at his sending for such a second,* said they were sure he would not come, that if they waited till he obeyed the summons, the affair would scarcely be decided in time for the masquerade, and many other provoking things of the same sort. They then departed, saying they should wait half an hour at the appointed place of meeting, but no longer. When the messenger returned, who said that Henry was at home and alone, and when a quarter of an hour passed without his appearing, the unfortunate Antonio, irritated extremely by the mockery of his opponents, and mortified beyond measure by the neglect of his friend, followed them to the place of rendezvous alone. The event has been already related. On hearing this melancholy story, Henry fell into an agony of despair: he had continually before his eyes the bleeding body of the dying Antonio, his last words for ever vibrated in his ears, and when he dozed for a moment, he was awakened by the sad speech, "Henry, I have then been mistaken." The agitation of his mind produced a violent attack of the jaundice, which lasted two months; a strong constitution and the best medical assistance enabled him to throw it off, but his mind received a wound which never could be entirely healed, and at that time he first experienced those fits of inquietude, anxiety, and restlessness, which many years after amounted to complete insanity.

As soon as he was able to take exercise, his physicians ordered him to travel, and in the course of some months, the change of scene had removed part of the heavy weight from his heart; he took some pleasure in the novelties that presented themselves to his observation, and in society sometimes appeared gay and thoughtless, but as he well remarked in his manuscript, "It often happens, that the momentary glow of animated conversation conceals the most deeply wounded spirit." He gave a long and entertaining account of his travels, with now and then an anecdote which shewed how little he had profited by the misfortunes brought upon him by his procrastinating temper. These however I do not recollect sufficiently to relate with accuracy, and shall therefore proceed to what I do remember.

After travelling two years in France and Spain, he returned home, and found his family in great affliction. His father had been attacked by a paralytic stroke the day before his arrival, and had not recovered either his speech or senses, and the physicians had no hopes of his life. Henry loved his father, who had ever been a most indulgent parent, with the strongest, truest affection; he was therefore sincerely grieved at finding him in this melancholy state, but his sorrow was not of that wild, outrageous sort, which he experienced on those occasions when he had to reproach himself with being the cause of the misfortune he deplored: and when his father, after lingering without sense ten days, at length ceased to exist, Henry was able to assist in consoling his mother, and to save her the trouble of looking over papers and arranging accounts.

By the death of his father, Henry came into possession of a large property, which the benevolence of his disposition would have led him to make a good use of, but his kindest intentions were frequently counteracted by the unconquerable indolence which governed him, and which must also have been the ruin of his commercial interests, had he not met with a series of extraordinary good fortune. In the manuscript were related a great number of melancholy stories of deserving persons who had been injured, by his sad propensity "to put off till to-morrow what ought to be done to-day." One only I shall mention, as it led to events of the greatest importance.

Amongst the many families in which Henry became intimate on his return from his travels, was that of Signor Pietro Lombardini, an old friend of his father, to whom he had rendered some important services in the early part of his life. His daughter Leonora bad been educated at the same convent with Louisa, where they were as remarkable for their attachment to each other, as for the many good qualities they possessed above their companions. Henry remembered to have seen Leonora, when he visited his sister in the parlour of their convent, and felt pleased in renewing his acquaintance with one whom he had thought so amiable. His partiality increased with his knowledge of Leonora's character, and in a short time a marriage between them was agreed on, to the universal satisfaction of the friends of both families. While preparations were making for the wedding, the father of Leonora (who was a great merchant) received the disagreeable intelligence that two of his ships from the Levant,* richly laden with the choicest commodities of the East, had foundered in a dreadful storm near the coast of Africa, and unfortunately he was so circumstanced at that particular time, as to have a large sum of money to pay down in a few days. His character and credit depended on punctuality in this business, and for the first time in his life he was obliged to have recourse to the kindness of his friends. Two of them immediately assisted him with the greatest alacrity; Henry was the third to whom he applied, and from him he naturally expected the most considerable aid. He had not at the moment a sufficient sum by him to answer the purposes of Signor Pietro, but with all that warmth of affection which he really felt, promised that the remainder should be ready on the day of payment. The old merchant, knowing the prosperous state of Henry's affairs, and the many claims which he had on his gratitude, as well as his attachment to his daughter, felt perfectly satisfied with this promise, and took no further trouble on the subject. Henry lost no time in arranging matters for procuring this money; he examined the accounts of sums due to him, considered who would be the person most proper to apply to, and determined to go to him next morning: but next morning he deferred going till too late, and thought a day's delay could be of no consequence, as the money was not to be paid for a week. In this manner he put it off from day to day, sometimes forgetting, and sometimes procrastinating, until the very day on which the money was to be paid. Early in the morning, the old merchant (who had hitherto refrained to mention it from motives of delicacy) wrote to remind him of his promise, which Henry recollected with much confusion: he then went to all the persons whom he had thought of, but unfortunately not one of these was able to supply him with so large a sum in a moment. He spent the whole morning in vainly seeking what a few days notice would have procured him without difficulty, and when he returned home in the afternoon, fatigued, disappointed, and ashamed of his ill success, he found a note from Leonora, intreating him, if he could not supply the money, at least to go to the hard-hearted creditor, and gain a little time for her father who was ill. For once in his life Henry made no delay. He went instantly, and employed every art of persuasion to induce the ill-natured man to accept of his security for the money being paid in less than a fortnight; but all to no purpose, for this second Shylock* was actuated more by malice than any other motive. The wretched Henry now discovered, that his procrastinating temper had thrown the friend of his deceased parent, the father of Leonora, into the power of an implacable enemy. In returning he passed by the house of Lombardini, but had not courage to enter it, and going home immediately, wrote a long and pathetic letter to his daughter, giving an account of his ill success, and endeavouring to deprecate* her anger.

Two hours having passed without an answer, Henry could no longer withstand his impatient anxiety; but on going to the house of Signor Pietro, he was informed that he expired half an hour before, and that his death proceeded from the bursting of a blood-vessel, occasioned by agitation of mind. Henry returned to his own house in a state of mind more easy to imagine than describe. In the morning he called to enquire after the Lombardini family. Day after day he was at their door, but could gain no admission; and at length the brother of Leonora wrote to request he would cease to give himself the trouble of coming to that house, as his sister could never think of marrying the man whose want of friendship to her father had been the cause of his death.

Whilst Henry was overwhelmed with grief at this severe disappointment, a person arrived from his mother's villa (about twenty miles from Leghorn), to say that she desired to see him immediately. The violence of his emotions prevented his attending to this message, and when it was repeated to him by his servant an hour after, he thought he might as well delay going till the next morning, forgetting that almost every hour since the death of Lombardini, he had repeated to himself that he never would procrastinate more. In the middle of the night, when all the inhabitants of Henry's house, except the unhappy master, were sunk in deep repose, a violent ringing at the gate roused them, and a messenger in a great haste announced, that if Henry wished to see his mother alive, he must instantly set out. As he had not taken off his clothes, he was soon ready to depart; but when he arrived, he found that his mother (who had been attacked by a fever a week before) had just ceased to exist, and that her last breath pronounced his name. This accumulation of misfortune was too much for his already disturbed intellects. He was immediately seized with the most dreadful insanity, and continued in that state upwards of two years. On his recovery he found that Leonora and Louisa had both taken the veil, and he determined to seek an abode in some new place, remote from the haunts of men. Such were the melancholy causes which drove him to that forest where we met him in such an extraordinary manner.

Here Daniel ended this sad story, which affected us all very much; but what affected us still more, was his declaration, that his stories were at an end till the month of May, when he hoped to resume them. I assure you some of us had tears in our eyes listening to this bad news. He tried to comfort us, by a promise that we should still have our treat of fruit or cakes; but I do not think there were three among us, who would not have been content to resign the eatables, if we could have retained the other part of our entertainment.

THE END

Fable of the Three Fishes

taken from

The Fool of Quality

THE

FOOL of Quality,

OR, THE

HISTORY

OF

HENRY

EARL of *Moreland*.

In FOUR VOLUMES.

By Mr. BROOKE.

DUBLIN:

Printed for the AUTOR.

By DILLON CHAMBERLAINE, in Dame Street,
facing Fownes's Street.
MDCCLXV

[By this stage of the novel, young Harry Moreland has made the acquaintance of a benevolent gentleman, Mr Fenton, who becomes his patron and oversees the boy's education; see also 'Introduction, p. 23.]

As *Harry*'s Ideas began to open and expand, he grew ambitious of greater Power and Knowledge. He wished for the Strength of that Bull, and for the Swiftness of yonder Horse. And, on the Close of a solemn and serene Summer's Evening, while he and his Patron walked in the Garden, he wished for Wings that he might fly up and see what the Sky, and the Stars, and the rising Moon were made of.

In order to reform this Inordinacy of his Desires, his Patron addressed him in the following Manner.

I will tell you a Story, my *Harry*. On the other Side of yonder Hill there runs a mighty clear River, and in that River, on a Time, there lived three silver Trouts, the prettiest little Fishes that any one ever saw. Now God took a great liking and love to these pretty silver Trouts, and he let them want for nothing that such little Fishes could have occasion for. But two of them grew sad and discontented; and the One wished for this Thing, and the Other wished for that Thing, and neither of them could take Pleasure in any Thing that they had, because they were always longing for something that they had not.

Now, *Harry*, you must know that all this was very naughty in those two little Trouts; for God had been exceedingly kind to them; he had given them every Thing that was fittest for them; and he never grudged them any Thing that was for their Good; but instead of thanking him for all his Care and his Kindness, they blamed him, in their own Minds, for refusing them any Thing that their silly Fancies were set upon. In short there was no End of their wishing, and longing, and quarrelling, in their Hearts, for this Thing and t'other.

At last, God was so provoked, that he resolved to punish their Naughtiness by granting their Desires, and to make the Folly of those two little stubborn Trouts an Example to all the foolish Fish in the whole World.

For this Purpose, he called out to the three little silver Trouts, and told them they should have whatever they wished for.

Now, the Eldest of these Trouts was a very proud little Fish, and wanted, forsooth, to be set up above all other little Fishes. May it please your Greatness, says he, I must be free to tell you that I do not, at all, like the Way in which you have placed me. Here you have put me into a poor, narrow, and troublesome River, where I am straitened on the right Side, and straitened on the left Side and can neither get down into the Ground, nor up into the Air, nor go where, nor do any one Thing I have a mind to. I am not so blind, for all, but that I can see, well enough, how mighty kind and bountiful you can be to Others. There are your favourite little Birds, who fly this Way and that Way, and mount up to the very Heavens; and do whatever they please, and have every Thing at Command, because you have given them Wings. Give me such Wings, also, as you have given to them, and then I will have something for which I ought to thank you.

No sooner ask than have. He felt the Wings he wished for growing from either Side, and, in a Minute, he spread them abroad, and rose out of the Water. At first he felt a wonderful Pleasure in finding himself able to fly. He mounted high into the Air, above the very Clouds, and he looked down with Scorn on all the Fishes in the World.

He now resolved to travel, and to take his Diversion far and wide. He flew over Rivers, and Meadows, and Woods, and Mountains; till, growing faint with Hunger and Thirst, his Wings began to fail him, and he thought it best to come down to get some Refreshment.

The little Fool did not consider that he was now in a strange Country, and many a mile from the sweet River, where he was born and bred, and had received all his Nourishment. So, when he came down, he happened to alight among dry Sands and Rocks, where there was not a Bit to eat, nor a Drop of Water to drink; and so there he lay faint and tired, and unable to rise, gasping, and fluttering, and beating himself against the Stones, till at length he died in great Pain and Misery.

Now, the second silver Trout, though he was not so high minded as the first little proud Trout, yet he did not want for Conceit enough, and he was moreover a narrow hearted and very selfish little Trout, and, provided he himself was snug and safe, he did not care what became of all the Fishes in the World. So he says to God:

May it please your Honour. I don't wish, not I, for Wings to fly out of the Water, and to ramble into strange Places, where I don't know what may become of me. I lived contented and happy enough, till the other Day, when, as I got under a cool Bank from the Heat of the Sun, I saw a great Rope coming down into the Water, and it fastened itself, I don't know how, about the Gills of a little Fish that was basking beside me, and he was lifted out of the Water, struggling and working in great Pain, till he was carried, I know not where, quite out of my Sight. So, I thought in my own Mind, that this Evil, some Time or other, may happen to myself, and my Heart trembled within me, and I have been very sad and discontented ever since. Now, all I desire of you, is, that you would tell me the Meaning of this, and of all the other Dangers to which you have subjected us poor little mortal Fishes; for then I shall have Sense enough to take care of my own

Safety, and I am very well able to provide for my own Living, I warrant you.

No sooner said than done. God immediately opened his Understanding; and he knew the Nature and Meaning of Snares, Nets, Hooks, and Lines, and of all the Dangers to which such little Trouts could be liable.

At first he greatly rejoiced in this his Knowledge; and he said to himself, now surely I shall be the happiest of all Fishes; for, as I understand and am forewarned of every Mischief that can come near me, I'm sure I love myself too well not to keep out of Harm's way.

From this Time forward, he took Care not to go into any deep Holes, for fear that a Pike, or some other huge Fish might be there, who would make nothing of swallowing him up at one Gulph.* He also kept away from the shallow Places, especially in hot Weather, lest the Sun should dry them up and not leave him Water enough to swim in. When he saw the Shadow of a Cloud coming and moving upon the River, a ha! said he to himself, here are the Fishermen with their Nets, and immediately he got on one Side and skulked under the Banks, where he kept trembling in his Skin, till the Cloud was past. Again when he saw a Fly skimming on the Water, or a Worm coming down the Stream, he did not dare to bite, however hungry he might be; no no, said he to them, my honest Friends, I am not such a Fool as that comes to neither; go your ways and tempt those who know no better, who are not aware that you may serve as Baits to some treacherous Hook, that lies hid for the Destruction of those ignorant and silly Trouts that are not on their Guard.

Thus, this over careful Trout kept himself in continual Frights and Alarms, and could neither eat, nor drink, nor sleep in Peace, lest some Mischief should be at Hand, or that he might be taken napping. He daily grew poorer, and poorer, and sadder, and sadder, for he pined away with Hunger, and sigh'd himself to Skin and Bone; till, wasted almost to nothing with Care and Melancholy, he at last died, for fear of dying, the most miserable of all Deaths.

Now, when God came to the youngest silver Trout, and asked him what he wished for. Alas (said this darling little Trout) you know, may it please your Worship, that I am but a very foolish and good for nothing little Fish; and I don't know, not I, what is good for me or what is bad for me; and I wonder how I came to be worth bringing into the World, or what you could see in me to take any thought about me. But, if I must wish for something, it is that you would do with me whatsoever you think best; and that I should be pleased to live, or die, even just as you would have me.

Now, as soon as this precious Trout made this Prayer in his good and his humble little Heart, God took such a Liking and a Love to him, as the like was never known. And God found it in his own Heart, that he could not but take great Care of this sweet little Trout, who had trusted himself so wholly to his Love and good Pleasure, and God went wheresoever he went, and was always with him and about him, and was to him as a Father and Friend and Companion; and he put Contentment into his Mind and Joy into his Heart; and so this little Trout slept always in Peace, and wakened in Gladness; and whether he was full or hungry, or whatever happened to him, he was still pleas'd and thankful; and he was the happiest of all Fishes that ever swam in any Water.

Harry at the Close of this Fable, looked down and grew thoughtful, and his Patron left him to himself to ruminate on what he had heard. Now, Harry had often heard talk of God, and had some general though confused Notions of his Power.

The next Day, he requested his Patron to repeat the Story of the Three little silver Trouts. When he had ended, Dada, says Harry, I believe I begin to guess a little at what you mean. You wouldn't have me wish for any Thing but leave every Thing to God; and, if I thought that God loved me, half as well as you love me, I would leave every Thing to himself, like the good little Trout. He does, my Harry, he loves you a thousand Times better than I love you, nay a thousand Times better than you love yourself. God is all Love; it is he who made every Thing, and he loves every Thing that he has made. Ay, but Dada, I can't, for the Heart of me help pitying the two poor little naughty Trouts. If God loves every Thing, why did he make any Thing to dye? You begin to think too deeply, Harry; we will speak more of these Matters another Time. For the present, let it suffice to know that, as he can kill, he can also make alive, again, at his own Pleasure.   ...

THE HISTORY

OF

Master *Billy Friendly*

AND HIS SISTER

Miss POLLY FRIENDLY

To which is added,

The FAIRY TALE of

THE

THREE LITTLE FISHES.

—————————

LONDON:

Printed and Sold by JOHN MARSHAL and Co.
at No. 4. Aldermary Church Yard, Bow-Lane.
[Price TWO-PENCE Bound and Gilt]

A

Curious and Instructive Tale

OF

THREE LITTLE FISHES.*

═══════════════════

ONCE upon a time, when fishes, birds, and beasts could speak, and when fairies had the power of doing what they pleased, it happened that a fairy sat down by the side of a fountain, where three little silver trouts were playing about the stream.——She took great delight in these little trouts, and came every day to look at them; till at last two of them grew uneasy at their situation, and when the fairy came again they desired that she would grant one wish to each of them.

Now this was a very naughty thing in the two little fishes, and you will see that they were rightly served for not being contented with their situation.

"What is it that you wish for? said the Fairy, if I can be of any benefit to you, you may depend upon it I will." So the eldest of these fishes wished that he might have wings like the *Birds*, that he might fly all over the world. Immediately the fairy touched him with her wand, and the wings grew from his shoulders, and he rose up out of the water, mounting into the air, above the very clouds.

He now resolved to travel, and to visit all the parts of the earth; he flew over rivers, woods, meadows, and mountains, till growing quite weary, he thought it best to come down, and take some refreshment. But the little fool forgot that he was in a strange country, and many a mile from the sweet fountain where he was born and fed. So when he came down, he happened to alight among dry sands and rocks where there was not a bit to eat, nor a drop of water to drink; and there he lay tired and unable to get up, fluttering and gasping, and beating himself against the stones, till at last he died in great misery.

Now the second of these two little fishes that was every bit as proud as his brother, desired that the fairy would change him into a Mouse: "Then (says he) I shall no longer be confined in a small narrow brook, but shall range about from place to place, just as I please; I shall feast upon the nicest things, and quench my thirst wherever I like."

Well——so it was; with a touch of the Fairy's wand, he directly became a *Mouse*, and instantly found himself in a pantry filled with dainties. But soon he heard a bustle at the door, and the cat was let in upon him, and forgetting every pleasure that he had before wished for, he wanted nothing now but to save his life. He ran about every where, and the cat pursued him whereso-ever he went, till after a chace of some time, he was at length taken, killed, and eat.

The Fairy then asked the youngest trout, whether he would wish for anything; but the good fish replied, "You know I am but a poor and silly fish, and I don't know what is good or bad for me; but if I must wish for something, it is that you would do with me what you think best; for I would like to live or die, just as you would have me."

Now, as soon as the little trout had said this, the Fairy took a great liking to him, and filled his heart with content and joy, so that this little trout slept always in peace, and awoke in gladness. Whenever he was hungry, the brook supplied him with food; and he swam with great delight about the brook, and whatever happened, he was always pleased and thankful, and was the happiest of all the little fishes that ever swam in the water.

APPLICATION.

This story of the fishes is a true picture of life, and if people were to be indulged in all their desires, they would bring nothing but distress, and ruin on themselves. Children should learn betimes to fear God, and to serve him rightly, and he will give them all that is proper for them, as he best knows what is for their good. If the two eldest fishes had been humble and content, they might have lived as happy as the youngest did, but by their own folly they were the means of bringing on their own destruction.

THE END.

THE

Three Little Fishes,

A STORY,

Intended for

THE INSTRUCTION OF YOUTH;

Together with an

Exhortation to the right Observance

OF

THE SABBATH DAY,

AND

A DISCOURSE ON THE BENEFIT OF

𝕾𝖚𝖓𝖉𝖆𝖞 𝕾𝖈𝖍𝖔𝖔𝖑𝖘.

Selected from the History of Harry Moreland.

Manchester:
PRINTED FOR A SOCIETY OF GENTLEMEN,
By Nanfan & Davis.

PRICE TWO-PENCE

TO THE

Children of the Sunday Schools,

IN THE

District of St. John's, Manchester.

———————

DEAR CHILDREN,

I HERE present you with a little Manual for your instruction, as a return for the satisfaction I have received from your late attendance at Church, to be instructed in your Church Catechism, and in the hope that you will find in it such further good advice, as may lead you to become good children and heirs of everlasting happiness. That you may profit by this, and by every other means of Grace, will be the sincere and constant prayer of your affectionate Pastor,

J. CLOWES.

St. John's, Jan. 19, 1801.

PART I.

The Three Little Fishes, &c.

———————•———————

HARRY MORELAND was a remarkable fine boy, and tenderly beloved by his parents, who conceived great hope from his virtues, that he would one day or other become a signal blessing to them. But young Harry, as he grew up, discovered manifest symptoms of discontent in his low situation in life, and expressed frequent wishes, in the presence of his parents, that he had been born to a better station, and been gifted with higher faculties than what he at present enjoyed.

His father one day observing this tendency in his son, and wishing to lead his young mind to cherish better sentiments, addressed him in the following manner:

I will tell you a Story, my Harry. — On the other side of yonder hill there runs a mighty clear river, and in that river, on a time, there lived three silver trouts, the prettiest little fishes that any one ever saw. Now God took a great liking and love to these pretty silver trouts, and he let them want for nothing that such little fishes could have occasion for. But two of them grew sad and discontented; and the one wished for this thing, and the other wished for that thing, and neither of them could take pleasure in any thing that they had, because they were always longing for something that they had not.

Now, Harry, you must know, that all this was very naughty in those two little trouts, for God had been exceedingly kind to them; he had given them every thing that was fittest for them; and he never grudged them any thing that was for their good; but, instead of thanking him for all his care and his kindness, they blamed him in their own minds for refusing them any thing that their silly fancies were set upon. In short, there was no end of their wishing, and longing, and quarrelling in their hearts, for this thing and t'other.

At last, God was so provoked, that he resolved to punish their naughtiness by granting their desires, and to make the folly of those two little stubborn trouts an example to all the foolish fish in the whole world.

For this purpose, he called out to the three little silver trouts, and told them they should have whatever they wished for.

Now, the eldest of these trouts was a very proud little fish, and wanted

[158]

forsooth to be set up above all little fishes. May it please your Greatness, says he, I must be free to tell you, that I do not at all like the way in which you have placed me. Here you have put me into a poor narrow and troublesome river, where I am straitened on the right side, and straitened on the left side, and can neither get down into the ground, nor up into the air, nor go where, nor do any one thing I have a mind to. I am not so blind, for all, but that I can see well enough, how mighty kind and bountiful you can be to others. There are your favourite little birds, who fly this way and that way, and mount up to the very heavens, and do whatever they please, and have every thing at command, because you have given them wings. Give me such wings also you have given to them, and then I will have something for which I ought to thank you.

No sooner ask than have. He felt the wings he wished for growing from either side, and, in a minute, he spread them abroad, and rose out of the water. At first he felt a wonderful pleasure in finding himself able to fly. He mounted high into the air, above the very clouds, and he looked down with scorn on all the fishes in the world.

He now resolved to travel, and to take his diversion far and wide. He flew over rivers and meadows, and woods and mountains; till, growing faint with hunger and thirst, his wings began to fail him, and he thought it best to come down to get some refreshment.

The little fool did not consider that he was now in a strange country, and many a mile from the sweet river where he was born and bred, and had received all his nourishment. So, when he came down, he happened to alight among dry sands and rocks, where there was not a bit to eat, nor a drop of water to drink: and so there he lay faint and tired, and unable to rise, gasping and fluttering, and beating himself against the stones, till at length he died in great pain and misery.

Now, the second silver trout, though he was not so high-minded as the first little proud trout, yet he did not want for conceit enough, and he was, moreover, a narrow-hearted and very selfish little trout, and provided he himself was snug and safe, he did not care what became of all the fishes in the world. So he says to God:

May it please your Honour, I don't wish, not I, for wings to fly out of the water, and to ramble into strange places, where I don't know what may become of me. I lived contented and happy enough till the other day, when, as I got under a cool bank from the heat of the sun, I saw a great rope coming down into the water, and it fastened itself, I don't know how, about the gills of a little fish that was basking besides me, and he was lifted out of the water struggling and working in great pain, till he was carried, I know not where, quite out of my sight; so, I thought in my mind, that this evil, some time or other, may happen to myself, and my heart trembled within me, and I have been very sad and discontented ever since. — Now, all I desire of you, is, that you would tell me the meaning of this, and of all the other dangers to which you have subjected us poor little mortal fishes: for then I shall have sense enough to take care of my own safety, and I am very well able to provide for my own living, I warrant you.

No sooner said than done. God immediately opened his understanding; and he knew the nature and meaning of snares, nets, hooks and lines, and of all the dangers to which such little trouts could be liable.

At first he greatly rejoiced at this his knowledge; and he said to himself, Now surely I shall be the happiest of all fishes; for, as I understand and am forewarned of every mischief that can come near me, I'm sure I love myself too well not to keep out of harm's way.

From this time forward he took care not to go into any deep holes, for fear that a pike, or some other huge fish, might be there, who would make nothing of swallowing him up at one gulph. He also kept away from the shallow places, especially in hot weather, lest the sun should dry them up, and not leave him water enough to swim in. When he saw the shadow of a cloud coming and moving upon the river, Aha! said he to himself, here are the fishermen with their nets, and immediately he got on one side, and skulked under the banks, where he kept trembling in his skin till the cloud was past. Again, when he saw a fly skimming on the water, or a worm coming down the stream, he did not dare to bite, however hungry he might be: no, no, said he to them, my honest friends, I am not such a fool as that comes to neither; go your ways and tempt those who know no better, who are not aware that you may serve as baits to some treacherous hook, that lies hid for the destruction of those ignorant and silly trouts that are not on their guard.

Thus this over-careful trout kept himself in continual frights and alarms, and could neither eat, nor drink, nor sleep in peace, lest some mischief should be at hand, or that he might be taken napping. He daily grew poorer and poorer, and sadder and sadder, for he pined away with hunger, and sighed himself to skin and bone; till, wasted almost to nothing with care and melancholy, he at last died, for fear of dying, the most miserable of all deaths.

Now, when God came to the youngest silver trout, and asked him what he wished for; Alas! (said this darling little trout) you know, may it please your Worship, that I am but a very foolish and good for nothing little fish; and I don't know, not I, what is good for me or what is bad for me; and I wonder how I came to be worth bringing into the world, or what you could see in me to take any thought about me. But if I must wish for something, it is that you would do with me whatsoever you think best; and that I should be pleased to live or die, even just as you would have me.

Now as soon as this precious trout made this prayer in his good and his humble little heart, God took such a liking and a love to him, as the like was never known. And God found it in his own heart, that he could not but take great care of this sweet little trout, who had trusted himself so wholly to his love and good pleasure; and God went wheresoever he went, and was always with him and about him, and was to him as a father, and friend, and companion; and he put contentment into his mind, and joy into his heart; and so this little trout slept always in peace, and wakened in gladness; and whether he was full or hungry, or whatever happened to him, he was still pleased and thankful; and he was the happiest of all fishes that ever swam in any water.

PART II.

On the Observance of the Lord's Day.

HARRY did not fail to profit by the advice concealed under his father's story, which, he had the good sense to see, was intended to make him content and thankful to GOD in his station in life. Nevertheless, though upon the whole a very good boy, and disposed at all times to listen to his Father's instructions, he was not quite so attentive to the duties of the Sabbath Day as his Father wished him; and one Sunday having been ordered to go to church by his parents, he was led astray by some of his young companions to spend the time in play, instead of attending the worship of GOD. His Father hearing of Harry's disobedience to his commands, and foreseeing the danger which would result from his carelessness about the duties of the Lord's day, took the opportunity, when they were alone together, of addressing him in the following words:

I am much concerned, my child, that you have so far disregarded my instructions, as to turn away from the Church of GOD, whither I had sent you, to mispend your time in idle sport and play. I wish, therefore, to remind you of the great sin which you have committed, and at the same time to impress, with the utmost solemnity, on your remembrance, this command of your GOD, "*Remember the Sabbath Day to keep it holy.*"

This is the command of the great God, the Maker of heaven and earth; "the God in whose hand thy breath is, and whose are all thy ways;"" the God who gave thee being; the God who gives thee all thy time, and who allows thee six days out of seven for worldly concerns. "Six days shalt thou labour and do all thy work; but the seventh day is the Sabbath of the Lord thy God."" He claims this day as his own. And can you refuse so just and equitable a claim? He has *hallowed* this day; that is, he has made it holy; he has reserved it for his own service; he has ordained, that from the beginning of the world to the end of it, the children of men should employ the sacred hours in holy acts of private or public worship.

Say now, is it not meet and right, and your bounden duty, cheerfully to obey the heavenly command? Consider how *necessary* and *reasonable* the appointment! It is necessary, were it only to give suitable rest to the bodies of men and beasts. Without this merciful institution, how many would have allowed neither themselves nor their servants proper seasons of repose. If there were no Sabbath in a nation, there would soon be no religion; and what then would become of the interests of morality? The merciful God appoints a Sabbath for *your* good. It is for your sake, not his own, that he requires it. He needeth not thee, nor any child of man. He seeks thy good, thy everlasting good; for he has not only *hallowed* this day, but he has also *blessed* it. It is a day of special grace. The King of heaven now sits upon his throne of mercy; he waits to be gracious; he gives audience to-day to all his faithful subjects. Millions of happy spirits now in heaven, will bless God to all eternity, for the spiritual blessings in Christ Jesus, which, when on earth, they received on this happy day; and thousands now on their way to glory, find it good for them to draw near to God, and justly esteem "a day in his courts better than a thousand."" So that you are an enemy to yourself, if you profane this day. If you love your own soul, why will you lose the opportunity of being happy?

If you studied only your *present* good, you would keep the Sabbath. God honours them that honour him. Many have found that a Sabbath, well spent, is usually followed by a prosperous week; for it is "the blessing of the Lord that maketh rich;"" and how can you expect his blessing, if you disobey him? Lord Chief Justice Hale* made the following observation: "I have found," said he, "that a due observing the duty of the Lord's day, hath ever joined to it a blessing upon the rest of my time; and the week that hath so begun, hath been blessed and prosperous to me: And on the other side, when I have been negligent of the duties of this day, the rest of the week hath been unsuccessful and unhappy to my secular employments.""

[162]

And, has not God frequently manifested his anger against Sabbath-break-ers? How many have perished in the midst of their amusements, and been suddenly called to the bar of God while engaged in actual rebellion against him! How many lovers of pleasure have been known, whose dying agonies have been awfully increased by the sad remembrance of the manner in which they spent former Sabbaths! And how many unhappy criminals have, in their last moments, ascribed their ruin to this sin. Beware, then, of a vice so dangerous in its tendency, so fatal in its consequences; for if you forsake God, he may justly forsake you, and then you are undone for ever.

Do you hope to go to heaven when you die? I know you do. But con-sider how the saints in glory are employed. They keep perpetual Sabbath, and the worship of God is their constant delight. But how can you reason-ably hope for heaven, unless you are *formed by grace for the business and pleas-ure of it*; and how could you enjoy an eternal Sabbath, who now turn your back upon God's worship, or say of the Sabbath, "What a weariness is it?"'

For God's sake, and for your own sake, "Consider your ways."' Let the time past suffice to have rebelled against your Maker. Rebel no longer. Now say, "Lord, it is enough. I have fought against thee too long. Forgive my iniquities past, and give me grace for time to come." No more let worldly business, nor vain amusements, engross these holy hours.

You must not rob God: the day is all his own. Let it be a *whole* day — a day as long as others. Say not, What harm is there in taking a little amuse-ment after divine service? Think a moment, and you will perceive the harm. Why should you *erase the impressions of holy things as soon as they are made*? Is not *retirement* as necessary as public worship? On other days much of your time is employed. Improve the leisure of a Sabbath. Retire and read your Bible. Converse with God in prayer. Converse with your own heart. Converse with good books. And, above all, be concerned to experience the blessings of the Gospel you hear. Have you been to church, and heard of the natural state of man as a sinner? Apply this to yourself, and be humbled in the dust of humiliation. Have you been told, from the word of God, that "Except a man be born again, he cannot see the kingdom of God?"' Enquire whether you have ever known a change of heart; and pray for the Holy Spirit in all his gracious influences, that you may be a new creature. Has some holy temper or moral duty been recommended to you from the pulpit? Endeavour to fix the necessity and beauty of it on your mind, that so you may bring it into practice. This is the way to keep a Christian Sabbath; and thus proceeding in the fear of God, you may humbly hope for God's bless-ing in the present world, and in the world to come.

PART III.

On the Benefit of Sunday Schools.

———————◆———————

YOUNG Harry listened with great earnestness to his father's discourse on the duties of the Sabbath Day, and was never known afterwards to be absent from Church on that day, unless prevented by sickness or other necessities. It was remarked also, that he always made a practice, on the evening of the Lord's Day, of retiring into his chamber, to spend some time by himself at his devotions, and in reading his Bible, or some other good and instructive book. Sometimes he would walk out with his father, who was a very good and pious man, though poor, and would attend him in his visits to some of his poor neighbours, whom his father was always happy to instruct as he saw occasion, that he might lead them to the knowledge of God, and of their duty. One day, when they were thus on a visit to a neighbouring family, the father observed several young children sitting about the fire, and began, as was his custom, to ask them a few questions, such as, whether they had been at Church? Whether they had been at the Sunday School? And what they had learnt there? Finding from their answers, that their Parents had been so careless, as never yet to send them to a Sunday School, he thought this a fit opportunity of expressing his sentiments on the subject to the Parents, and accordingly, in the presence of Harry and the rest of the children, he thus accosted them.

It is a great mercy that God has given you children, and has preserved both you and them to this time. How many women are cut off in childbirth!* How many fathers and mothers are torn from their helpless babes! Multitudes of infants pine away and die before the eyes of their weeping parents.* Many children are born blind, or deaf and dumb: and some turn out idiots, without common sense to learn, or do anything to get their bread. How kind, then, has the Lord been to you! —— Though you are poor, he has given you health to work, or friends to help you; so that you and your children have been kept from starving. Now he is graciously providing for the good of their minds, by inclining people to teach them to read the Bible. As you cannot teach them yourselves, nor can pay to have them taught, how thankful should you be to the Lord for putting it into the heart of any body else, to do so much good to your children. It will cost us some money, and time, and trouble; and we are not kin to you, nor expect any reward from you; but we are willing to do this for God's sake, who has taught us to love our neighbours as ourselves. If you love your children, you will be very glad to use such means to do them good.

By sending them to the Sunday School, you may do them great good, and keep them from much harm. Don't you find, that if your children have nothing to do, they get into mischief? When they play about in the streets, they are apt to learn the bad words, and bad behaviour, of the worst children they meet with. They get into quarrels and danger; and then perhaps come home and tell you lies. They won't mind what you say to them, nor do as you would have them. They are not thankful nor dutiful to you now; and what may you expect when they grow up? Is it not likely, and almost certain, that they will get worse and worse, if they are not taught better, and kept out of harm's way? What can you do with them on a Sunday so well as to send them to worship God, and to be taught to read their Bible? This will shew them how wrong it is for them to lie, or swear, or steal, or disobey their parents. It will shew them that God is angry with children who do such things, and that he will even turn them into Hell if they go on doing so. If they come to know and mind what the Bible tells them, you won't have the trouble to scold and beat them in order to keep them from doing what is wrong. They will remember that God always sees them, and they will be afraid of displeasing him.

On the other hand, if they have not the fear of God before their eyes, you do not know what end they may come to. How common is it for young people to be led to commit crimes that ruin them for ever! There is not a week passes without some being taken up, and put in prison. Every now and then numbers are executed at the gallows; and ships, loaded with criminals, are sent to Botany Bay.* What should hinder your children from taking the same course that so many fall into, if they are not kept from temptation, and taught what is right while they are young? Most poor young creatures that come to be hanged say, that they began to be ruined by not keeping the Sabbath. And how can your children be hindered from this sin, but by being sent to a Sunday School, and by attending public worship? Whether they are able or not to work at any thing the rest of the week, you cannot and ought not to make them work on the Lord's day. The fourth commandment says, "Remember the Sabbath Day to keep it holy; In it thou shalt not do any work; thou, nor thy son, nor thy daughter."* If you cannot teach your children yourselves, the only way likely to keep them from wicked courses, is to send them to a Sunday School.

Doing this, is likely not only to keep them from harm, but also to do them good. If they mind what they are taught in the Bible, they will behave well to you and to every body. The persons who are so kind as to attend to their learning, will take notice of them, and may be glad to employ them as they grow up, or recommend them to others who can provide better for them. Many poor children have come to be rich and greatly respected, by getting learning and behaving well; and your's are as likely to do so as others. So they will become more dutiful and useful to you while they are children, but when they become men and women, and you are old and feeble, they will be glad to support and comfort you, and may be able to make your last days the happiest in your lives.

If there was no future life, and no other world but this in which to live, it would be much for your own and your children's interest, that they should read and mind the Bible. Among the people you are acquainted with, how much better those are off who are decent, sober, honest, and diligent; than those who are idle, drunken, lewd, and dishonest! But the Bible is *God's book*. It was written by persons who knew and loved God, and all that they say is true. It teaches us, that there is another life after this; and that they who know and love God in this world, will go to Heaven, while they who will not learn and do his will, must go to Hell. You and your children will be sure to go to one or other of these places when you die, and will there be happy or miserable for ever. Now, how shocking it will be if you and they should be together in Hell; and they should tell you, "this is because you did not teach us better, nor let others teach us, who wished to do so! you, who brought us into the world, have brought us to *Hell* by your neglect and bad examples". —— But how charming it would be for you to see your children in *Heaven*, and hear them bless God for having given them parents who taught them to love and serve him!

Are you ready to weep at these thoughts? "Yes," perhaps you say, "but what good can that do? I am not fit to go to Heaven, nor my children neither. Young as they are they have already learned much evil; and they are so perverse, that I have no hope that they will get better." Too many parents have reason to make this complaint, and too few are aware of it. If this is *your* case, it is bad indeed; but the Bible teaches us the only way to escape the wrath to come. It tells us that *Jesus Christ* came to save sinners, that he died for them, and that all who believe on him shall have everlasting life. Hence it is that Saint Paul wrote to young Timothy, "from a child thou hast known the Holy Scriptures, which are able to make thee wise unto salvation."* Neither you nor your children can be saved without knowing the Holy Scriptures. If you read them you will see this to be true; and you will see that God gives his *Holy Spirit* to them who ask him. If any one of you cannot read, you are much to be pitied; but you may hear the Scriptures explained and preached; and if you do not, you will go to hell without excuse. But what a happy thing it is, that the Lord provides means for your children to learn better. The Lord Jesus Christ said, when he was upon earth, "Suffer little children to come unto me, and forbid them not.'" What wretches must those parents be who will not suffer their children to come to Christ? And how can they come to Christ if they do not learn the Scriptures, which teach us who he is, what he has done and suffered for us, and how we may be saved through his mercy?

If your children wish to learn these things, you must be monsters of cruelty indeed to hinder them. But you cannot expect them to know what is good for themselves, if you do not tell them. They are likely to love play more than learning, but if you let them have their own way in every thing, you will be sure to ruin them, and to make them torments to yourselves. Whereas, if you take care always to send them to the Sunday School at the proper hours, they will soon get the habit of going, and of obeying you in other things. If any body would hinder you from sending them to learn the Bible, you may be sure, after what has been said, they are not your friends, but enemies both to you and your children, whatever they may pretend. You need not fear *them* if you please *God*. Think of all the *harm* that is likely to befal you and your children, if you do not send them to learn the Bible; and of all the *good* that you and they may gain by doing so. —— Bless God that he has inclined any body to teach them; send them early and constantly to learn; and take care to do and say nothing that would hinder the blessed effects of it for this life and that which is to come. May the grace of our Lord Jesus Christ be with you and yours!

P.S. Any well-wisher to Parents who cannot read this Address, is requested to read it to them.

Notes

Learning better than House and Land

Title page *LEARNING BETTER THAN HOUSE AND LAND*: variations on the phrase were proverbial; see Samuel Foote, *Taste* (London, 1752), p. 12: 'as the old Saying is, When House and Land are gone and spent, then Learning is most excellent'; David Garrick, 'Prologue', in Oliver Goldsmith, *She Stoops to Conquer; or, The Mistakes of a Night* (London, 1773), n.p.: 'Learning is better far than house and land'; Maria Edgeworth, *Castle Rackrent: an Hibernian Tale* (London, 1800), pp 18–19: '[the] old proverb, "learning is better than house or land"'.

Title page *AS EXEMPLIFIED IN THE HISTORY OF A 'SQUIRE AND A COW-HERD*: The subtitle in subsequent editions changed to *AS EXEMPLIFIED IN THE HISTORY OF HARRY JOHNSON AND DICK HOBSON*.

Title page *J. CAREY, LL.D.*: For John Carey, see Introduction above, pp 10–12. Carey is known to have studied at a French university, but it is unclear which institution awarded his doctorate in law.

Title page *B. TABART AND CO*: Benjamin Tabart was the publisher of the second edition of 1810. The third edition of 1813 and the fourth undated edition (1824?) were also published in London by William Darton. Both firms were associated with the production of popular and improving children's books.

p. 34 *various other publications*: John Carey's previous publications included *Profitable amusement for children; or, Puerile tales, uniting instruction with entertainment* (London, 1802); *The works of Virgil: translated into English verse, by John Dryden*, 3 vols (London, 1803); *Scanning Exercises for Young Prosodians; containing the first two epistles from the Electa ex Ovidio, minutely scanned and proved by the Rules of the Eton Grammar, and interspersed with occasional remarks* (London, 1807).

p. 34 *translator of several works from the French*: John Carey's obituary in *The Gentleman's Magazine*, January 1830, 376, records: 'He translated the following works: The Batavians, from the French of Mons. Bitaubé, The Young Emigrants, from Madame de Genlis'. No extant copies of these translated works have been identified.

p. 34 *His* SHORT-HAND *may separately be learned in four Lessons*: Carey's system of shorthand was based on that devised by the American, Thomas Lloyd. A teacher, stenographer and acquaintance of Mathew Carey (1760–

1839), the Philadelphia-based printer, bookseller, and philanthropist, Lloyd began to record the debates of the Pennsylvania Assembly in the late 1780s, announcing in 1791 that henceforth this work would be printed from short-hand notes jointly taken by himself and John Carey, Mathew's older brother. Two years later, John Carey published *The System of Short-hand, practised by Mr. Thomas Lloyd, in taking down the debates of Congress; and now (with his permission) published for general use* (Philadelphia, 1793); see Marion Tinling, 'Thomas Lloyd's Reports of the First Federal Congress', *The William and Mary Quarterly*, Third Series, 18:4 (Oct. 1961), 519–45.

p. 34 *a new edition of his* 'Latin Prosody made easy': The first edition of *Latin Prosody made easy; or, Rules and Authorities for the Quantity of final Syllables in general, and of the Increments of Nouns and Verbs, interspersed with occasional Observations and Conjectures on the Pronunciation of the ancient Greeks and Romans, to which are added Directions for scanning and composing different Kinds of Verse, followed by analytic Remarks on the Harmonious Structure of the Hexameter, together with Synoptic Tables of Quantity for every Declension and Conjugation* was published by Robinsons in London in 1800. The prefatory material in the new, improved and enlarged edition of 1808, published by Longmans, advises that the author 'has just published a Moral Tale for Youth, entitled *"Learning better than House and Land"*.'

p. 34 *Approved ... July 16, 1808*: This page does not feature in the third edition (1813) or the fourth edition (1824?). In the second edition (1810), it is preceded by the following prefatory information:

Opinions of Reviewers on
"LEARNING BETTER THAN HOUSE AND LAND".

This little tale inculcates the best moral principles, and is sufficiently interesting to attract the attention of youth. The incidents ... (&c.) ... present impressive examples, which cannot fail to be advantageous to young minds, and, as such, we recommend it. The talents of Dr. Carey are well known: the principles of morality, here exemplified, are no less honourable to him.

Anti-Jacobin Review, November, 1808.

As the moral of these juvenile performances is the main object, the more pleasing the story combined with it, the more instruction it is likely to convey. This little work intends to describe the solid advantages which may be derived from learning; and, to make them more apparent, the author gives us a little tale, in which two families are portrayed with some ingenuity......so that the maxim of learning being *"better than house and land"* is exemplified in the vicissitudes of Harry Johnson and Dick Hobson.

Critical Review, December, 1808.

Publications by Dr. Carey,
to be had of W. Darton, 58, Holborn Hill.

Practical English Prosody and Versification, or Descriptions of the different species of English Verse, with Exercises in Scanning and Versification, gradually accommodated to the various Capacities of Youth at different Ages, and calculated to produce Correctness of Ear and Taste, in reading and writing Poetry.

   Key to Practical English Prosody and Versification.
   Latin Prosody, a new and improved edition.
   Abridgement of the same, for schools.
   Scanning Exercises for young Prosodians.
   Alphabetic Key to Propria quae Maribus, &c.
   Skeleton of the Latin Accidence.
   Dryden's Virgil, revised and corrected.

He has now in the press Poetic Reading made easy, or a Selection of Poetry for Schools, with directions for the proper utterance of each line.

This prefatory material, with the exception of the final reference to *Poetic Reading*, was retained in the 1813 edition.

p. 35 *An Apology*: the second edition (1810) retains Carey's prefatory observations as presented here. The third edition (1813), however, opens more briefly under the heading 'Advertisement' in place of 'Apology': 'IN offering this artless tale to the public, I am well aware …' before continuing as previously. In the undated fourth edition (1824?), the corresponding material, announced as 'PREFACE TO THE FIRST EDITION', contains some substantive variations to both the first and third editions, as detailed below in notes to pp 35 and 37.

p. 35 *pupil*: The undated fourth edition (1824?) replaces 'pupil' with its French equivalent '*élève*'; Carey dedicated the 1808 edition of *Latin Prosody Made Easy* to Spencer Perceval (1762–1812), then Chancellor of the Exchequer, and later Prime Minister, in which office he was assassinated. In the dedication, Carey mentions the three years he spent tutoring the Chancellor's son, suggesting that one of Perceval's offspring may have been the youth in question.

p. 35 *bolts of Jove*: The king of the Roman gods, Jove, or Jupiter, controlled the skies and was believed to unleash bolts of thunder when displeased.

p. 35 *bounds of truth*: At this point in the undated fourth edition, Carey adds the following footnote: 'I have only described it as I actually found it many years since.—Whether any change have since taken place for better or for worse, I leave to be told by those who have more recently visited the United States. *October*, 1823'.

p. 35 *encomium*: Expression of praise.

[171]

p. 35 *Martinsburg and Winchester*: Founded in 1778 by General Adam Stephen, Martinsburg is a city in present-day West Virginia; Winchester, originally Frederickstown but renamed in 1752, lies to the south of Martinsburg, and served as George Washington's headquarters when he commanded Virginia's troops during the French and Indian War of 1754–63.

p. 36 *the plantation ... a negro*: As in other American states, the plantation system of Virginia depended on the labour of slaves imported from the West Indies and Africa, until this practice was officially prohibited in 1808 by Article I, Section 9 of the United States Constitution.

p. 37 *nineteen years*: The second edition (1810) retains this reference to the passing of nineteen years, while adding 'July 16, 1808' at the end of Carey's introductory remarks, indicating that his meeting with the Perry family took place in 1789. The prefatory material, dated July 1813, in the third edition (1813), changes the reference to 'twice twelve years', again indicating that the events recounted occurred in 1789. The fourth edition (1824?) substitutes 'neither time nor distance' for the earlier, more precise detail.

p. 37 *J. C.*: The undated fourth edition (1824?), in which the preface to the first edition is reproduced, substitutes John Carey for J. C. and provides 1 July 1808 as the date of composition of these introductory remarks. That new information is followed by a short note:

> Having already had the gratification of witnessing three very numerous editions of this simple but instructive tale, I now, again, for the fourth time, commit it to the press, with a well-founded hope that it may still continue to enjoy the public approbation.
>
> J. C.
>
> *October* 15, 1823.

p. 38 *Berkeley Square*: laid out *c.*1730 by the architect William Kent (*c.*1685–1748), Berkeley Square was, and is, a fashionable residential area in the West End of London, in the City of Westminster.

p. 38 *landed property*: Such a property generates income for an owner who does not carry out any of the work on the estate, and may reside elsewhere.

p. 38 *a seat in parliament for a borough belonging to the estate*: Mr Johnson benefitted from the electoral system which, prior to the 1832 Reform Act, allowed powerful landowners to gain unrepresentative influence within Parliament. In *Vindiciae Hibernicae* (Philadelpia, 1819), p. 241, Mathew Carey, John Carey's younger brother, argued: 'The borough system in England has gradually become the scourge of that nation, and the astonishment and disgust of the rest of the world'.

p. 38 *avocations*: Incidental employments.

p. 39 *vengeance is mine*: Romans 12:17.

p. 39 *who willeth ... and live*: The phrase, from Ezekiel 18:23, was common in prayers, sermons and devotional tracts throughout the eighteenth century.

p. 39 *tedious and expensive process in Chancery*: The court of the Lord High Chancellor of England, where property cases were determined according to principles of fairness or equity instead of the strict principles of common law, was renowned for being inefficient and costly.

p. 40 *surety*: Here, guarantor.

p. 40 *Three hundred pounds are but a scanty pittance*: At a time when the average annual income of a clergyman was £120, and all who earned more than £60 were liable for tax, £300 was not an insubstantial sum; see T.V. Jackson, 'British Incomes circa 1800', *Economic History Review*, 52:2 (1999), 257–83. Mathew Carey emigrated to Philadelphia with £25 in his pocket; see Mathew Carey, *Autobiography* (New York: E.L. Schwaab, 1942), p. 9.

p. 40 *drawn pictures ... flatter him*: Carey anticipates the view of his brother, the art critic William Paulet Carey, that 'a good portrait painter never wanted encouragement in this country'; William Paulet Carey, *Letter to L*** A******, *esq. a Connoisseur in London* (London, 1809), p. 24.

p. 40 *brook*: Endure.

p. 41 *an assortment of cutlery ... handsome profit*: Silver cutlery, imported from England, was a symbol of status in Virginia in the late-eighteenth century, so represented a form of portable wealth for travellers.

p. 41 *for which place he set sail*: Ships regularly sailed from Deal, Clowes, and Plymouth for Philadelphia during the eighteenth century, the transatlantic voyage generally taking approximately two months. Mathew Carey, for example, left Dublin on board the *America* on 7 September, 1784, and landed in Philadelphia on 1 November 1784; see Mathew Carey, *Autobiography*, p. 9. The number of English emigrants to America increased in the decades following the War of Independence (1775–83); see Marilyn C. Baseler, *Asylum for Mankind: America, 1607–1800* (Ithaca, NY: Cornell University Press, 1998), pp 156–8.

p. 41 *a beautiful phænomenon ... diminished size*: Marine rainbows, as described here, had been reported as early as 1694 by John Narborough, *An account of several late voyages & discoveries to the south and north towards the Streights of Magellan, the South Seas, the vast tracts of land beyond Hollandia Nova &c.* (London, 1694) p. 49; in 1797 Charles Taylor described the phenomenon, 'termed a sea-bow, i.e. the prismatic colours refracted from the spray of the waves', to young readers as follows:

> To produce this, the sea must run high enough to afford a good deal of dashing spray; and the sun must, (as in a rain-bow) be behind the spectator, but as it seldom happens, that when the sea runs so high the sun shines out clear, these phenomena are rarely noticed. The principles of this bow are the same as those of the rain-bow, but as many bows are seen at once, each wave making one, the sight is extremely curious.

Charles Taylor, *The general genteel preceptor: by Francis Fitzgerald, Esq. being a summary introduction to polite learning. Adapted to the service and instruction of youth of both sexes, And of Others, who wish to acquire, or to confirm, useful and pleasing Knowledge in the various Branches of Education*, 3 vols (London, 1797), ii, p. 95.

In a letter to the *Monthly Magazine*, 27:1 (1809), 140, Carey explained that the wording of this passage had been changed immediately prior to publication to avoid suggesting that '*every* wave on *every* side represented a rainbow'. The description of the phenomenon was further refined in the third edition (1813):

> On this occasion, they did co-operate:—the wind blowing pretty fresh, and from the proper point, to throw the spray into an advantageous position—the sun shining extremely bright, and obliquely darting his rays on the bursting waves, in such direction, as to form, with the spectator's eye, the exact angle requisite to produce the wondrous effect—innumerable small rainbows were seen at once starting up to view, and vanishing, in rapid succession—all within a limited space in the quarter opposed to the sun—where the showery spray of each wave, as tossed from its curling top by the wind, offered to the astonished sight the momentary exhibition of a perfect rainbow, though of diminished size (pp 25–6).

The undated fourth edition retains this amended description.

p. 42 *an empty quart bottle … pores of wood*: Similar experiments had been described from as early as 1680; see John Lowthorp, *The philosophical transactions and collections, to the end of the year 1700. Abridg'd and dispos'd under general heads*, 3 vols (London: 1716), i, p. 521. Interestingly, because of the Philadelphia connection, a variation of this experiment was reported by Benjamin Franklin (1706–90) in a letter published four years before his death:

> On the 14th of August the following experiment was made. The weather being perfectly calm, an empty bottle, corked very tight, was sent down 20 fathoms, and it came up still empty. It was then sent down again 35 fathoms, when the weight of the water having forced in the cork, it was drawn up full; the water it contained was immediately tried by the thermometer, and found to be 70, which was six degrees colder than that at the surface.

'A letter from Dr. Benjamin Franklin to Mr. Alphonsus le Roy, member of several Academies, at Paris. Containing Sundry Maritime Observations', *Transactions of the American Philosophical Society, Held at Philadelphia, for Promoting Useful Knowledge*, 2 vols (Philadelphia, 1786), pp 284–329, p. 329.

p. 42 *Delaware bay*: A major estuary outlet of the river Delaware, the entrance to this bay lies approximately eighty seven nautical miles to the south of Philadelphia.

p. 42 *the old Congress who had first voted the independence of America*: The Second

Continental Congress adopted the United States Declaration of Independence in the Pennsylvania State House, now known as Independence Hall, in Philadelphia on 4 July 1776.

p. 42 *federal hall*: Federal Hall, built in 1700 as New York's City Hall and later the site of George Washington's 1789 inauguration as the first President of the United States, was demolished in 1812.

p. 42 *Kentucky*: Kentucky, which became the fifteenth state to be admitted to the union, in June 1792, was a popular destination for migrants after the War of Independence (1775–83).

p. 42 *Congress*: The United States Congress, consisting of the Senate and the House of Representatives, was established under the Philadelphia Convention of 1787.

p. 43 *he thought it his duty … suicide*: In the posthumously published essay, 'On Suicide' (1783), David Hume (1711–76) outlined and sought to refute prevailing views of suicide as sinful, criminal and cowardly.

p. 44 *Martial … daring to live*: From Martial's *Epigrams* (XI, LVI, ll 15–16), the lines in the footnote translate: 'In misfortune it is easy to despise life. He is truly brave who can endure misery'; Carey introduced the first line of the quotation in the 1808 improved edition of *Latin Prosody made Easy*, p. 60, when discussing the plural increment of nouns.

p. 44 *Azores, or Western Islands*: Settled by the Portuguese in the fifteenth century, the island group lies some 2600 km south-west of London, 1800 km west of the African coast, and 4000 km east of the American coast.

p. 44 *a dire alternative … driven*: Narratives, such as *A true account of the voyage of the Nottingham-Galley of London* (London, 1711) and *The Shipwreck and Adventures of Monsieur Pierre Viaud* (Dover, NH, 1799), did much to establish and strengthen connections between shipwreck and cannibalism in the popular imagination.

p. 45 *oakum*: Loosely twisted fibres, often obtained by unpicking old hemp rope, used as a caulking material for the seams of wooden ships.

p. 45 *dog-days*: The hottest, sultriest period of the year, reckoned in antiquity from the rising of Sirius, the Dog Star.

p. 46 *seised*: i.e., seized.

p. 46 *neither mutes nor hearses nor mourning-coaches*: During the long eighteenth century, elaborate, formal funerals became indicators of high social status in England; see Julian Litten, *The English way of death: the common funeral since 1450* (London: Hale, 1991).

p. 48 *village school*: The years leading up to 1770 witnessed the establishment throughout England of a number of village schools, supported by the voluntary contributions of the villagers, which aimed to teach poor children to read and write.

p. 48 *Whittington's history*: This story, loosely based on the life of the merchant and mayor of London, Richard Whittington (c.1350–1423), had circulated since the beginning of the seventeenth century in both oral and print forms, with many chapbook versions being produced throughout the eighteenth century. Arguing against the deleterious effect of fairy tales which suggested that success in life depended upon magical intervention rather than hard work, Oliver Goldsmith claimed in 1759 that 'the old story of Whittington might be ... serviceable to the tender mind, were his cat left out'; see Washington Irving (ed.), *The Miscellaneous Works of Oliver Goldsmith; with an Account of his Life and Writings* (Philadelphia: J. Crissy, 1838), p. 456. Here, Harry's focus on Whittington's attentive industry suggests that he, probably unknowingly, concurs with Goldsmith's sentiments.

p. 50 *he had hopes ... read and write*: Stephen Brumwell, *Redcoats: the British soldier and war in the Americas, 1755–1763* (Cambridge: Cambridge University Press, 2002), p. 82, notes that promotion to the rank of corporal or sergeant was conditional on a candidate being able to read and write 'in a tolerable manner'. The Regimental School System, introduced by the duke of York in 1811, was the first official provision made for the education of common soldiers and their children.

p. 50 *the American war*: The American War of Independence (1775–83).

p. 50 *a reduced gentleman*: i.e., a gentleman in reduced circumstances.

p. 51 *perquisites*: Casual sources of income.

p. 52 *steerage*: Those parts of a merchant ship, usually in the bow and on a lower deck, allotted to passengers who travelled at the cheapest rate and could not afford a cabin.

p. 53 *the Chinese unscrupulously feed on the flesh of animals that have died a natural death*: The belief that Chinese willingness to eat animals that had died a natural death provided evidence of cultural inferiority was widespread; see, for example, George Henry Mason, *The Costume of China, illustrated by sixty engravings: with explanations in English and French* (London, 1800), plate VII, n.p.

p. 54 *They had not been ... fowls or other delicacies*: Bearing the title, 'Nautical Anecdote', the extracted story of the strange, onboard mortality among the fowls was published in the January 1810 edition of *The Lady's Magazine*.

p. 54 *regales*: Sumptuous feasts.

p. 55 *quarter-deck*: That part of the upper deck of a ship reserved for the use of superior officers and privileged passengers.

p. 55 *yard-arm*: The outer portion of the spar supporting the square sail on a mast.

p. 57 *five rows of strong sharp teeth*: Of the multiple rows of teeth possessed by an adult shark, only the first row or two are actively used for feeding, the remaining rows being made up of replacement teeth in various stages of formation.

p. 57 *clowns*: Rustics, peasants.

p. 57 *gobbets*: Large lumps or mouthfuls of food.

p. 57 *the number and maker's name*: To avoid theft and prevent the production of substandard fakes, pocket watches were engraved with the name of the maker and a serial number in the closing decades of the eighteenth century.

p. 57 *cipher and crest*: The initials of the owner's name worked into a design along with his family crest.

p. 57 *Besides these ... was drowned*: See note below to p. 00.

p. 58 *a poor harmless porpoise ... notice of approaching storms*: For the proverbial foreboding of a storm by a porpoise, see Morris Palmer Tilley, *A Dictionary of the Proverbs in England in the Sixteenth and Seventeenth Centuries* (Ann Arbor, MI: University of Michigan Press, 1950), p. 483.

p. 58 *the forecastle*: The forward part of the ship.

p. 58 *the "Shipwreck"*: First published in 1762, *The shipwreck. A poem. In three cantos. By a sailor*, was soon revealed to be the work of Edinburgh born William Falconer (1732–69). Telling the story of the disastrous final journey of the merchant ship *Britannia* from Alexandra to Venice, which only three of the crew survived, the poem was a huge popular success, leading to is reissue in new, improved and corrected editions, including one published in Philadelphia in 1788.

p. 58 *"the fleetest coursers of the finny race." CANTO 2, 217*: The line as quoted and numbered, which did not feature in early editions of the poem, appeared in the fourth, corrected edition published in Dublin in 1777, and in subsequent editions published elsewhere.

p. 59 *soundings*: Shallow waters.

p. 60 *Long-Island*: Bounded on the south by the Atlantic Ocean and separated from Manhattan by the East River, Long Island lies east of New York City.

p. 60 *yawl*: Small rowing boat.

p. 61 *the newspaper*: The *Minerva*, New York's first daily newspaper was established by Noah Webster in 1793; *Greenleaf's New Daily Advertiser* ran from 1796 to 1800.

p. 64 *a doubloon*: A Spanish gold coin.

p. 65 *compting-house*: i.e., counting-house.

p. 65 *which are only thirty-six pounds sterling*: The third (1813) and fourth (1824?) editions replace this phrase with a footnote that reads: 'Thirty-three pounds, fifteen shillings, sterling; the intrinsic value of the dollar being four shillings and six pence'.

p. 68 *an apprentice-fee*: A sum paid to cover the costs of training a youth in a profession or trade.

p. 68 *washy, water-gruel, smock-faced*: Feeble, insipid, effeminate.

p. 68 *Miss Molly*: Slang for an effeminate young man; see Francis Grose, *A classical dictionary of the vulgar tongue* (London, 1788), n.p.

p. 68 *caudles*: Warm drinks given as restoratives to invalids.

p. 68 *slops*: Here, semi-liquid food for invalids.

p. 68 *he was accordingly bound*: i.e., he was accordingly indentured to Mr Dapperly to learn his master's trade.

p. 69 *ebriety*: Drunkenness.

p. 69 *Hopson ... associate*: Dick changes his name to Hopson to remove indication of his own status as the son of a 'hob': i.e., a clown or rustic.

p. 70 *Within less than eighteen months ... great cloak and portmanteau*: In the third edition (1810), this account of Dick's success is considerably expanded, to include his election to Congress:

> Within less than eighteen months after his admission into the partnership, Mr Harvey gave him his daughter in marriage, with a very handsome portion; and Mr. Hopson, as we must henceforth call him, now enjoyed a fair prospect of making a rapid and immense fortune. His commercial dealings were extensive: and, as he exerted uncommon diligence in the execution of his plans, which were formed with consummate judgement, he was blessed with good success in every enterprise, insomuch that, within the course of a few years, he became one of the most opulent merchants in America.
>
> Conspicuous as he was for his wealth, he was still more distinguished by the good qualities which marked his character and conduct, and was so universally esteemed and respected by the citizens of New York, that, without any solicitation on his part, they spontaneously elected him as their representative in the Congress—that celebrated assembly, in which men of various religions are seen sitting together in friendly union; no one inquiring what his neighbour's tenets are; since the American Constitution admits no distinction on account of religion; but, with an enlightened and liberal policy, has left even the highest offices in the republic equally, accessible to men of every persuasion, without requiring any other religious test, than the bare profession of their '*belief in the existence of a God, and a future state of retribution;*' which belief the Americans have experimentally found sufficient for all the purposes of social life, and for the due and conscientious discharge of every public duty—leaving it to each individual to believe, in other respects, according to the convictions of his own mind—and justly considering, that belief is not an act of the will—that a man cannot believe as he chooses—and that the taking of a test-oath, when interest is concerned, is not always a proof of conviction, or a security for the punctual performance of the duty undertaken.†
>
> The seat of government having, about the time of Mr. Hopson's election, been transferred from New York to Philadelphia, he repaired to the latter city, to take his seat in Congress, at the commencement of the session: and how different from his first arrival at New York was his present entry into Philadelphia!—in the former case, a poor, disconsolate orphan, on foot—now, an opulent, high-minded legislator, riding an excellent horse of his own, and attended by a servant equally well mounted, who carried his master's great cloak and portmanteau.

A footnote, dated *July* 30, 1813, given below, follows 'undertaken' above:

†The passage with quotation-marks is copied from a short essay of mine in favor of *universal religious equality*, which I have long and ardently wished to see established by law in the British empire—fully convinced that it would here produce the same happy effects which I have personally witnessed from it in America.—In declaring this opinion (not hastily adopted during the late discussion of the Catholic question, but deliberately formed at a very distant period of my life, and ever since invariably and uniformly expressed both in conversation and writing) I am not influenced by any personal or party consideration, or by any other motive, than a perfectly disinterested Christian desire of *'doing unto all men as I would they should do unto me'*—a wish to see religion freed from all shackles, and every man enjoying his natural right to worship God agreeably to the dictates of his own conscience, without being subject to any penalties or disadvantages on account of his creed. My little essay, above mentioned, was published in the Lady's Magazine for April, 1811, under the title of *'Bigotry and Intolerance.'*

Despite Carey's assertion, this essay did not appear in any number of the *Lady's Magazine* published in 1811. The fourth edition of *Learning better than House and Land* (1824?), reproduces this expanded account of Dick's rise in life, but replaces the footnote above with another, as follows:

†Perfectly and signally consonant to that undiscriminating spirit of religious toleration was the conduct of the Federal Congress, in their choice of chaplains, on their meeting in Philadelphia in the year 1791. The Senate appointed one—the House of Representatives another—the one an Episcopalian Protestant—the other a Dissenter,—if the appellation of *"Dissenter"* can, with propriety, be applied to any man in the American Union, where there exists no state religion, from which he could be said to *dissent.*—However that may be, these chaplains officiated alternately in each of the two houses, a week each time; so that, where the Episcopalians read prayers during one week, the Dissenter prayed during the week ensuing: and thus they regularly continued to alternate throughout the entire session (pp 134–5).

p. 70 *a hired post-chaise*: A horse-drawn, four-wheeled carriage, bearing up to two passengers and mail.

p. 70 *stages*: The most common form of communal transport before the introduction of steam powered railways to the United States in the 1820s, stage-coaches were four-wheeled, closed vehicles, drawn by four horses, usually bearing six passengers and goods. They made regular stops at stages or stations as they ran between major towns and cities.

p. 70 *the Jerseys*: The provinces of East and West Jersey that made up the state of New Jersey.

p. 72 *Whene'er a dislike … gentleman barber*: The same moral could be applied to the experience of an illiterate French barber, who is said to have been murdered because he intercepted a message from the mysterious late-seventeenth century prisoner known as 'the man in the iron mask'; see *A new geographical, commercial, and historical grammar; and present state of the several empires and Kingdoms of the world*, 2 vols (Edinburgh, 1790), II, p. 575.

p. 73 *Poplar*: A metropolitan borough in the East End of London.

p. 73 *Dodsley's Annual Register … lost at sea two years before*: An account of a shark taken in the Thames, whose stomach contents included the watch of a young gentleman then identified by the maker's mark, much to the anguish of the youth's bereaved father, appeared in *The annual register, or a view of the history, politics, and literature, for the year 1787* (London: J. Dodsley, 1789), p. 227.

Stories of Old Daniel

Title page Emblem: This highly unusual emblem combines apparently contradictory elements: the helm of Britannia, also familiar as the helm of Minerva, is placed above Britannia's shield, perhaps signifying wisdom and martial prowess, but the wand to the left shows the French revolutionary cap of liberty while Mercury's wand suggests the peaceful resolution of conflict; the plant to the left is bay or laurel, used to crown victors and poets, while that to the right is palm, signifying either or both victory and peace.

Title page *Juvenile Library … Snow-Hill*: The Juvenile Library, founded by William Godwin and his second wife, Mary Jane Clairmont, in Hanway Street in 1805, moved to 41 Skinner Street in 1807; see also 'Introduction', p. 17. The collection was printed by Richard Taylor and Co. of Shoe-Lane. This firm was run by the printer and naturalist, Richard Taylor (1781–1858), who went on to become one of the founding partners of Taylor and Francis publishing house in 1852.

p. 79 *Old Daniel*: This character is said to be based on a retired soldier who lived in Kingston College, a home for elderly Church of Ireland gentlemen and gentlewomen in reduced circumstances, founded by James King, 4th baron of Kingston, in 1760; see Janet Todd, *Daughters of Ireland: the Rebellious Kingsborough Sisters and the Making of a Modern Nation* (New York: Ballantyne, 2004), p. 65.

p. 79 *I do not perceive … vulgar or provincial phrases*: That authors should avoid vulgarity when addressing children was a given. A critic of the second edition of John Carey's *Profitable Amusement for Children* (1818), for example, remarked: 'We would say to this writer, and to all who compose books for children, "Be thou familiar but by no means vulgar"'; *The Monthly Review* (May 1819), 105.

p. 79 *little foretastes … elder years*: As indicated in the author's footnote, the phrase is taken from Charles Lamb's preface to *Tales from Shakespear*, 2 vols (London, 1807), i, p. v.

p. 83 *doated*: i.e., doted.

p. 83 *elbow chair*: i.e., armchair.

p. 83 *jessamine*: i.e., jasmine.

p. 87 *taught by a foolish maid-servant … sort of things*: John Locke's condemnation of servants who 'awe Children, and keep them in subjection, by telling them of *Raw-Head* and *Bloody-Bones*', *Some Thoughts concerning Education* (London, 1693), p. 159, was echoed by later influential commentators, including Mary Wollstonecraft and Maria Edgeworth; see Celestina Wroth, '"To Root the Old Woman out of Our Minds": Women Educationists and Plebeian Culture in Late Eighteenth-Century Britain', *Eighteenth-Century Life*, 30:2 (2006), 48–73.

p. 88 *When I … first went into the army*: His childhood and enlistment were later described in 'Old Daniel's own story', *Continuation of the Stories of Old Daniel* (London, 1820), pp 158–80.

p. 89 *constables*: Military officers.

p. 90 *lanthorn*: i.e., lantern.

p. 91 *hunt the hare*: A traditional running game in which one child, the hare, tries to elude the other participants; see Joseph Strutt, *The Sports and Pastimes of the People of England* (London, 1867), p. 381.

p. 95 *north of Ireland*: One of the chief seats of the Mount Cashell family was at Galgorm Castle in the northern Irish county of Antrim; see *The Peerage of England, Scotland, and Ireland*, 3 vols (London, 1790), iii, p. 170.

p. 95 *linen business*: The northern province of Ulster was the centre of the eighteenth-century linen industry in Ireland; see W.H. Crawford, *The impact of the domestic linen industry in Ulster* (Belfast: Ulster Historical Foundation, 2005), pp 59–104.

p. 95 *trowsers*: i.e., trousers.

p. 95 *wear petticoats till he was thirteen*: While young children of both sexes wore petticoats, boys usually progressed to wearing breeches around the age of seven, so that breeching was an important eighteenth-century rite of passage.

p. 96 *cloaths*: i.e., clothes.

p. 98 *at the bar*: i.e., in the courts of law.

p. 99 *gaming*: In a pamphlet discussing divorce rates and the education of young Englishmen, gaming was described as a 'dreadful vice' to which 'every misfortune which has lately fallen on this country [could] be attributed'; see *Hints for a reform, particularly in the gambling clubs. By a Member of Parliament* (London, 1784), p. 10.

p. 100 *knee-buckles*: Ornamental fastenings to hold breeches tightly above or below the knee.

p. 104 *banditti*: Gangs of bandits. Lady Mount Cashell feared such marauders on the European tour she began in 1801; see Thomas Sadlier, (ed.), *An Irish Peer on the Continent (1801–1803); Being a Narrative of the Tour of Stephen, 2nd Earl Mount Cashell, through France, Italy, Etc, as related by Catherine Wilmot* (London, Williams and Northgate, 1920), pp 86, 106, 117.

p. 104 *chaise*: Carriage.

p. 104 *postillion*: Rider of the horse drawing a carriage.

p. 106 *called in Italy* stilettos: Signifying a small dagger, the term 'stiletto' was in general English usage by 1800.

p. 107 *Sbirri*: The police force of the Papal States in central Italy was distrusted and generally dreaded by the Italian populace; see John Adams, *Anecdotes, bons-mots, and characteristic traits of the greatest princes, politicians, philosophers, orators, and wits of modern times* (Dublin, 1789), pp 254–5.

p. 109 *lottery*: following the suppression of private lotteries in 1709, they came under state control. Between 1769 and 1820, thirty state lotteries offering prize funds of up to £600,000 were held; see C. L'Estrange Ewen, *Lotteries and sweepstakes; an historical, legal, and ethical survey of their introduction, suppression and re-establishment in the British Isles* (London: Heath Crampton, 1932), pp 199–213.

p. 111 *ballads*: Broadside ballads, generally printed on one side of poor quality paper, and chapbooks containing ballads, were popular commodities, purchased by all strata of eighteenth-century society.

p. 112 *a dog … hot iron*: Scarification of the wound, followed by treatment with a hot iron, was the recommended remedy for the bite of a rabid dog; see John Allen, *Synopsis medicinæ: or, A summary view of the whole practice of physick*, 2 vols (London, 1740), i, p. 221.

p. 113 *post-house*: Inn.

p. 115 *cave*: While staying in an inn in Fontainebleau in 1802, Lady Mount Cashell and her companions heard the story of 'an old Hermit with a long white beard who inhabits a cavern in the forest, where he has dwelt some six and thirty years … to expiate some sins of his youth'; see Sadlier (ed.), *An Irish Peer on the Continent*, p. 88.

p. 115 *I always deferred … done today*: That what could be done today should not be deferred until the morrow was proverbial; see Morris Palmer Tilley, *A Dictionary of the Proverbs in England in the Sixteenth and Seventeenth Centuries* (Ann Arbor, MI: University of Michigan Press, 1950), T378.

p. 117 *half-holiday*: A day of which the latter half is taken as a holiday.

p. 117 *a sad custom … that country*: 'Modern Duels began and were first indulg'd in France', and continued to take place there despite being outlawed by Louis XIII in 1626; see John Cockburn D.D., *The History and Examination of Duels. Shewing their Heinous Nature and the Necessity of Suppressing them* (London, 1720), p. 343.

p. 117 *botanizing*: Studying plants. In *The Mysteries of Udolpho, a Romance*, 4 vols (London, 1794), i, p. 21, Anne Radcliffe described how Monsieur St Aubert amused himself botanizing in the foothills of the Pyrenees.

p. 118 *the saint's day whose name he bore*: An individual's name-day was defined as 'the day of the saint a person bears the name of'; see Thomas Deletanville, *A new French dictionary, in two parts* (London: 1794), n.p.

p. 118 *patroles*: i.e., patrols.

p. 119 *herbal*: Book containing notes on herbs and other plants.

p. 120 *two monstrous bears*: From the middle of the nineteenth century, hunting depleted the Pyrenean brown bear population, leading to the protection of the species in 1973 and the introduction from 1995 of Slovenian bears to boost the native stock.

p. 122 *Grotto del Cane*: Situated on the shore of Lake Agnano, this cave was frequently mentioned by geographers and travel writers; see, for example, Adam Alexander, *A Summary of Geography and History, both Ancient and Modern* (Edinburgh, 1794), p. 154, and Mariana Starke, *Letters from Italy, between the years 1792 and 1798, containing a view of the revolutions in that country, from the capture of Nice by the French Republic to the expulsion of Pius VI. from the ecclesiastical state* (London, 1800), pp 154–5. In 1803, Lady Mount Cashell visited the cave and 'saw the effects of the carbonic acid on a dog', see Sadlier, (ed.), *An Irish peer on the continent*, p. 157.

p. 122 *a poor animal … on his mercy*: For an account of a similar rescue of a dog by the duke of Hamilton, see William Mavor, LL.D., *Historical account of the most celebrated voyages, travels, and discoveries, from the time of Columbus to the present period* (London, 1797) pp 113–14.

p. 123 *a large, deserted-looking house*: In Pavia in 1802, Lady Mount Cashell and her travelling companions 'were disabled from going any further than a few miles by the torrents of rain that fell, and therefore were oblig'd to put up at a miserable wild dismantled looking house, with all the air in the world of being haunted, either with Spirits or Banditti'; Sadlier, (ed.), *An Irish Peer on the Continent*, p. 117.

p. 124 *scribbling on different parts of the walls*: The inn room in which Lady Mount Cashell slept in Pavia had 'warnings scrawled with blood and charcoal against the wall'; Sadlier, (ed.), *An Irish Peer on the Continent*, p. 118.

p. 126: *one of the sons*: Lady Mount Cashell's party learned of the inn's 'being not only a harbour for assassins, but of the landlord and his sons being privy to the murders and sharing in the plunder'; Sadlier, (ed.), *An Irish Peer on the Continent*, pp 119–20.

p. 129 *flatter*: Here, encourage, cheer.

p. 130 *serjeants*: i.e., sergeants.

p. 132 *Leghorn*: A Tuscan port on the Ligurnian Sea, Leghorn, or Livorno, was enlarged and opened up to foreign merchants by Leopold II (1747–1792). Katherine Wilmot, who visited the town with Lady Mount Cashell in 1803, judged it 'one of the best Maritime Ports on the Mediterranean'; Sadlier, (ed.), *An Irish Peer on the Continent*, p. 195.

p. 132 *prevented*: Anticipated.

p. 136 *sopha*: i.e., sofa.

p. 137 *rally*: Tease.

p. 137 *second*: Assistant to a duellist.

p. 139 *the Levant*: Countries east of the Mediterranean.

p. 140 *Shylock*: Moneylender in Shakespeare's *The Merchant of Venice*, entered on the Stationers' Register in 1598 and first printed 1600.

p. 140 *deprecate*: Here, seek to ward off.

The Fool of Quality, or, The History of Henry Earl of Moreland

Title page *DILLON CHAMBERLAINE in Dame Street*: This Dublin printer and bookseller was renowned for his publication of the first or early editions of well-received novels, including the first two volumes of Laurence Sterne's *Tristram Shandy* in 1760. His firm moved from its original premises in Smock Alley to 38 Dame Street in 1765; see Mary Pollard, *A dictionary of members of the Dublin book trade 1550–1800: based on the records of the Guild of St Luke the Evangelist Dublin* (London: Bibliographical Society, 2000), pp 98–9.

p. 149 *Gulph*: i.e., gulp.

The History of Master Billy Friendly, and his Sister Miss Polly Friendly: to which is added, the Fairy Tale of the Three Little Fishes

Title page *JOHN MARSHAL and Co.*: The son of a chapbook printer, John Marshall (*c*.1755–*c*.1825) was renowned for borrowing or adapting works published by other firms, and for his cavalier attitude to dating his own publications.

p. 153 *A Curious and Instructive Tale OF THREE LITTLE FISHES*: This version of Brooke's fable bears no relation to two stories which precede it in the anonymously authored *The History of Master Billy Friendly, and his Sister Miss Polly Friendly: to which is added, the Fairy Tale of the Three Little Fishes*. The first story recounts how young Billy Friendly lives an exemplary life and becomes a very rich man, while the second tells how his equally virtuous sister, Polly, marries a rich man and becomes a fine lady; see also 'Introduction', pp 24–5.

The Three Little Fishes, A Story, Intended for the Instruction Of Youth, Together with an exhortation to the right Observance of the Sabbath Day, And A Discourse On the Benefit of Sunday Schools.

Title page *Sunday Schools*: Associated with Robert Raikes (1735–1811), the Sunday School movement, which began in the 1780s, provided classes in religion and literacy for the working children of the poor.

p. 162 *Remember the Sabbath Day to keep it holy*: Exodus 20:8; the remainder of 'Part II. *On the Observance of the Lord's Day*' appeared anonymously as Tract 14 in *The Publications of the Religious Tract Society Vol. 1* (London, 1801).

p. 162 *the God in whose hand … thy ways*: Daniel 5:23.

p. 162 *Six days … Lord thy God*: Exodus 20:9–10.

p. 162 *a day … a thousand*: Psalms 84:10.

p. 162 *the blessing … maketh rich*: Proverbs 10:22.

p. 162 *Lord Chief Justice Hale*: Matthew Hale (1609–1676) was called to the bar in 1636, knighted in 1671, and appointed chief justice of the king's bench in 1671.

p. 162 *I have found … secular employments*: See Matthew Hale, *Contemplations Moral and Divine*, 2 vols (5th ed. London, 1792), i, p. 430.

p. 163 *What a weariness is it*: Malachi 1:13.

p. 163 *Consider your ways*: Haggai 1:7.

p. 163 *Except a man … kingdom of God*: John 3:3.

p. 164 *women cut off in child-birth*: The maternal mortality rate per 10,000 births in England in 1800 has been estimated as being as high as 280; see Irvine Loudon, *Death in childbirth: an international study of maternal care and maternal mortality, 1800–1950* (Oxford: Clarendon Press, 1992), p. 159.

p. 164 *Multitudes of infants … weeping parents*: The infant mortality rate has been estimated at just below 200 per 1000 in 1800; see Eilidh Garrett et al., *Infant mortality: a continuing social problem* (Aldershot: Ashgate, 2007), p. 6.

p. 165 *Botany Bay*: From 1788 to 1823, Botany Bay in New South Wales served as a penal colony for convicts transported from the British Isles. In 1801, the age of criminal responsibility was seven. While there are no national statistics on the number of juveniles executed or transported before the mid-1830s, one hundred and three death sentences were passed on children for theft at the Old Bailey alone between 1801 and 1836. None, though, was eventually executed, with the sentence sometimes being commuted to transportation; see V.A.C. Gatrell, *The Hanging Tree: Execution and the English People 1770–1868* (Oxford: Oxford University Press, 1994), p. 2, n. 5; p. 215.

p. 165 *Remember … thy daughter*: Exodus 20:8–10.

p. 166 *From a child … unto salvation*: 2 Timothy 3:15.

p. 167 *Suffer little children … forbid them not*: Matthew 19:14; Luke 18:16.

List of emendations

The present text follows the spelling and punctuation of the first edition of *Stories of Old Daniel: or Tales of Wonder and Delight*, with the exception of the few emendations listed below.

p. 116, l. 13: singulard welling] singular dwelling
p. 122, l. 11: satisfies her:] satisfies her:"
p. 131, l. 10–11: ou school-room] our school-room
p. 135, l. 17: Felix.] Felix."
p. 139, l. 2 up: hard-harted] hard-hearted

The present text of 'A Curious and Instructive Tale of Three Little Fishes' follows the spelling and punctuation of pages 37–44 of the undated *The History of Master Billy Friendly, and his Sister Miss Polly Friendly: to which is added, the Fairy Tale of the Three Little Fishes*, with the one exception listed below.

p. 153, l. 1 up: like.] like."

The present text follows the spelling and punctuation of *The Three Little Fishes, a Story, intended for the Instruction of Youth: together with an Exhortation to the Right Observance of the Sabbath Day, and a Discourse on the Benefit of Sunday Schools. Selected from the History of Harry Moreland*, with the few exceptions detailed below.

p. 160, l. 22: clould] cloud
p. 160, l. 16 up: houest] honest
p. 161, l. 5: could but] could not but

Select bibliography

PRIMARY TEXTS

[Anon]. *The History of Master Billy Friendly, and his Sister Miss Polly Friendly: to which is added, the Fairy Tale of the Three Little Fishes*. London: John Marshal, n.d. [1787?].

Brooke, Henry. *The Fool of Quality; or, The History of Henry, Earl of Moreland*. Printed for the Aut[h]or. Dublin: Dillon Chamberlaine, 1765.

Carey, John. *Learning better than House and Land, as exemplified in the History of a 'Squire and a Cow-herd*. London: B. Tabart, 1808.

——. *Learning better than House and Land, as exemplified in the History of Harry Johnson and Dick Hobson*. London: B. Tabart, 1810.

——. *Learning better than House and Land, as exemplified in the History of Harry Johnson and Dick Hobson*. London: W. Darton, 1813.

——. *Learning better than House and Land, as exemplified in the History of Harry Johnson and Dick Hobson*. London: W. Darton, n.d. [1824?].

Clowes, John. *The Three Little Fishes, a Story, intended for the Instruction of Youth: together with an Exhortation to the Right Observance of the Sabbath Day, and a Discourse on the Benefit of Sunday Schools. Selected from the History of Harry Moreland*. Manchester: Nanfan & Davis, 1801.

Moore, Margaret King [Lady Mount Cashell]. *Stories of Old Daniel: or Tales of Wonder and Delight*. London: Printed for the Proprietors of the Juvenile Library, 1808.

——. *Stories of Old Daniel: or Tales of Wonder and Delight*. London: M.J. Godwin, 1810.

——. *Stories of Old Daniel: or, Tales of Wonder and Delight*. A new and improved edition. London: M.J. Godwin, n.d. [1820?].

SECONDARY TEXTS

a) Stories and authors included in the volume

Compton, Theodore. *The Life and Correspondence of the Reverend John Clowes, M.A: formerly fellow of Trinity College, Cambridge, and rector for sixty-two years of St. John's, Manchester*. London: 1882.

Donovan, Kevin Joseph. 'The Giant-Queller and the Poor Old Woman: Henry Brooke and the Two Cultures of Eighteenth-Century Ireland', *New Hibernia Review*, 7:2 (2003), 107–20.

McAleer, Edward. *The Sensitive Plant: A Life of Lady Mount Cashell*. Chapel Hill, NC: University of North Carolina Press, 1958.

Markey, Anne. 'Irish Children's Fiction 1727–1820', *Irish University Review*, 41:1 (2011), forthcoming.

—. 'The English governess, her wild Irish pupil, and her wandering daughter: migration and maternal absence in Georgian children's fiction', *Eighteenth-Century Ireland/Iris an dá chultúr*, 26 (2011), 160–75.

Mavor, Elizabeth (ed.). *The Grand Tours of Katherine Wilmot*. London: Weidenfeld and Nicholson, 1992.

Myers, Mitzi. 'Gendering the "Union of Hearts": Irish Politics between the Public and Private Spheres', *Studies in Eighteenth-Century Culture*, 30 (2001), 49–70.

Scheuermann, Mona. '"More than "A Few Passages": Henry Brooke's *The Fool of Quality* as the source for Thomas Day's *The History of Sandford and Merton*', *Durham University Journal*, 58 (1983), 55–9.

—. *Social Protest in the Eighteenth-Century English Novel*. Columbus: Ohio State Univ. Press, 1985. Pp. 41–68.

Todd, Janet. 'Ascendancy: Lady Mount Cashell, Lady Moira, Mary Wollstonecraft and the Union pamphlets', *Eighteenth-Century Ireland/Iris an dá chultúr*, 18 (2003), 98–117.

—. *Rebel daughters: Ireland in conflict 1798*. London: Viking, 2003.

b) Childhood and children's books

Ariès, Phillipe. *Centuries of Childhood: A Social History of Family Life*, trans. Robert Baldick. 1960; New York: Vintage Books, 1962.

Barnard, Toby. 'Children and Books in Eighteenth-Century Ireland', in Charles Benson and Siobhán Fitzpatrick (eds), *That Woman!: Studies in Irish Bibliography: A Festschrift for Mary 'Paul' Pollard*. Dublin: Library Association of Ireland Rare Books Group and the Lilliput Press, 2005. Pp 213–38.

—. 'Fiction available to and written for cottagers and their children', in Bernadette Cunningham and Máire Kennedy (eds), *The Experience of Reading: Irish Historical Perspectives*. Dublin: Rare Books Group of the Library Association of Ireland and Economic and Social History Society of Ireland, 1999. Pp 124–72.

Bottigheimer, Ruth B. 'An Important System of Its Own: Defining Children's Literature.' *Princeton University Library Chronicle*, 59 (1998), 191–210.

Cunningham, Hugh. *Children and Childhood in Western Society since 1500*. London: Longman, 1995.

Grenby, M.O. 'Children's Literature: Birth, Infancy, Maturity', in Janet Maybin and Nicola J. Watson (eds), *Children's Literature: Approaches and Territories*. Basingstoke & Milton Keynes: Palgrave Macmillan & Open University, 2009. Pp 39–56.

Grenby, M.O. and Andrea Immel (eds). *The Cambridge Companion to Children's*

Literature. Cambridge: Cambridge University Press, 2009.

Hilton, Mary, Morag Styles and Victor Watson (eds). *Opening the Nursery Door: Reading, Writing and Childhood 1600–1900*. London: Routledge, 1997.

Hilton, Mary and Jill Sheffrin (eds). *Educating the Child in Enlightenment Britain: Beliefs, Cultures, Practices*. Aldershot: Ashgate, 2009.

Hunt, Peter (ed.). *International Encyclopedia of Children's Literature*, 2 vols. London: Routledge, 2004.

——. *Children's Literature: An Illustrated History*. Oxford: Oxford University Press, 1995.

Immel, Andrea and Witmore, Michael. *Childhood and Children's Books in early modern Europe, 1550–1800*. London: Routledge, 2006.

Myers, Mitzi. 'Impeccable Governesses, Rational Dames, and Moral Mothers: Mary Wollstonecraft and the Female Tradition in Georgian Children's Books', *Children's Literature*, 14 (1986), 31–56.

Nikolajeva, Maria. *Children's Literature comes of Age: Towards a New Aesthetic*. New York: Garland, 1996.

Nodelman, Perry. *The Hidden Adult*. Baltimore, MD: Johns Hopkins University Press, 2008.

O'Malley, Andrew. *The Making of the Modern Child: Children's Literature and Childhood in the late Eighteenth Century*. London: Routledge, 2003.

Pollock, Linda. *Forgotten Children: Parent-child Relations from 1500 to 1900*. Cambridge: Cambridge University Press, 1983.

Richardson, Alan. *Literature, Education, and Romanticism: Reading as Social Practice, 1780–1832*. Cambridge: Cambridge University Press, 1994.

Rose, Jacqueline. *The Case of Peter Pan, or, the Impossibility of Children's Fiction*. Basingstoke: Macmillan, 1994.

Shavit, Zohar. 'The Historical Model of the Development of Children's Literature' in Maria Nikolajeva (ed.), *Aspects and Issues in the History of Children's Literature*. Westport, CT: Greenwood Press, 1995. Pp 27–38.

Stephens, John. *Language and ideology in children's fiction*. London: Longman, 1992.

Trumpener, Katie. 'Tales for Children', in Richard Maxwell (ed.), *The Cambridge Companion to Fiction in the Romantic Period*. Cambridge: Cambridge University Press, 2008. Pp 177–90.

Wall, Barbara. *The Narrator's Voice: the Dilemma of Children's Fiction*. Basingstoke: Macmillan, 1990.